BEYOND
ANGER

BEYOND ANGER

a guide for men

How to Free Yourself from the Grip of Anger and Get More Out of Life

Thomas J. Harbin, Ph.D.

Marlowe & Company
New York

Published by
Marlowe & Company
An Imprint of Avalon Publishing Group Incorporated
245 West 17th St., 11th Floor
New York, NY 10011

Grateful acknowledgment is made to R. W. Novaco for permission to reprint the
Novaco Provocation Inventory.

*The information in this book is intended to help readers make informed decisions
about their health and the health of their loved ones. It is not intended to be a
substitute for treatment by or the advice and care of a professional healthcare
provider. While the author and publisher have endeavored to ensure that the
information presented is accurate and up to date, they are not responsible for
adverse effects or consequences sustained by any person using this book.*

Library of Congress Cataloging-in-Publication Data
Harbin, Thomas J., 1954–
    Beyond anger : a guide for men : how to free yourself from the grip of anger and
get more out of life / by Thomas J. Harbin
        p. cm.
    Includes bibliographical references and index.
    ISBN 1-56924-621-1
    1. Anger   2. Men—Psychology.   I. Title

    BF575.A5.H345 2000
    152.4'7'081—dc21   99-052782

Editors: Ellen Cavalli, Jill Metzler, Shannon L. Donovan
Production: Janine Lehmann
Cover and interior design: Janine Lehmann
Typesetting: Janine Lehmann
Cover photograph © Sips Image—Leo de Wys, Inc.

19 18 17 16 15 14 13 12 11 10
Printed in the United States of America
Distributed by Publishers Group West

For Mimi,
of my soul.

contents

This is a book that I had to write. I had to write it for two reasons. First, I needed some materials to give to my patients, men who have a problem dealing with their anger. But writing this book also helped me organize my thoughts and feelings about the role of anger in my own life. Many years ago, others had told me that I had a problem with anger, but I didn't take them seriously. In fact, I may never have been motivated to take this look at myself if I had not come close to ruining the most important thing in my life: my marriage.

On our 10th wedding anniversary, my wife told me that "if the next 10 years are going to be like the last 10 years, I'm outta here." Her words were not spoken in anger, but there was no doubt that she meant what she had said. What I had seen as a very good marriage with occasional arguments, she had seen as a constant, heavy burden. She felt as though she was always walking on eggshells so as not to "set me off." When we had a disagreement, I brooded about it for days. Any time she disagreed with me, I immediately went on the attack and tried to defeat her and her point of view by almost any means. When she told me that she had taken all that she could stand, I took her seriously and decided that I had to do some frank soul searching to keep from losing the most important person I had ever known.

It was not until I was in my early thirties—a time when a lot of men become introspective and really begin to take stock of themselves and their lives—that I began to take this critical look at myself. As part of that process, I began to compare myself and my reactions to those of other people. Most people seemed to have more fun than I did. Things didn't seem to bother them as much. They seemed to have more friends and closer friends. I began to realize that what I felt was not what most people felt. Unlike me, most people woke up and started their days looking forward to what life would bring—or at least not actively dreading it. I, on the other hand, approached most days from the perspective of surviving. I was rarely optimistic. I could not enjoy the successes that I did have because I was constantly worrying about what bad things *might* happen. I always assumed that things would go wrong, and if things were going to go wrong, it was better to fall from a low height (unhappiness) than from a greater height (happiness or satisfaction).

I had no idea that what I felt was different from what others felt. I assumed that anyone who was optimistic was either ignorant about the "realities" of the world or was a hypocrite. I noticed that other families hugged and kissed each other frequently and casually, while I was never very comfortable with this kind of outward display of affection; it was shocking to me to realize that these people were not being phony. It hit me like a ton of bricks when I realized that they truly loved each other, were comfortable showing their love to each other, and that I had been missing out on a huge chunk of life. It's only looking back now that I can see I was afraid to put my emotions out there because I was afraid of humiliation and rejection.

My anger got in the way of almost all forms of enjoyment. I couldn't spend money on myself and resented it when my wife spent reasonable amounts on the things that she needed and wanted. I could not handle even mild criticism without getting angry. I turned minor disagreements into major arguments by taking everything too seriously. Though I did have some fun and though I was able to act relaxed and confident when circumstances demanded it, *I was always angry.*

As I look back, many of my habitual ways of dealing with the world were driven by anger. I was an aggressive driver, using my horn and my "freeway finger" whenever people weren't driving the way I thought that they should. If a mechanic told me that something needed to be fixed on my car, I was sure that he was exaggerating for his own financial gain. I thought that I had an unusual ability to see through a hypocrite—and since I thought that most people were hypocrites, I got a lot of practice at seeing through them!

All of these tendencies were not helped by my first career as a researcher and teacher. In order to be hired as a researcher at a university, you have to distinguish yourself from all of the other bright and extremely competitive professionals. This usually involves an almost constant process of putting your ideas out there and having your colleagues try to shoot them down. Almost anyone would find constant criticism upsetting, but to an angry man it means constant humiliation.

My second career as a practicing psychologist and therapist developed at about the same time that I began working on my own anger. I decided to develop a specialty in treating angry men, and I soon realized I needed a book for them to read. I admired Harriet Lerner's book for women, *The Dance of Anger* (HarperPerennial, 1997), and thought that it was the best self-help book ever written. But there was no book for angry men that I found to be as useful. This became my second reason for writing this book. I wrote two or three chapters and began giving them to my angry male patients. I gradually added to it one chapter at a time, and the results of my labor are what you see here.

Now, a decade later, I can honestly say that I am no longer the man I used to be. I am much more able to enjoy myself. I am not nearly as reluctant to let down my guard and let people see the inside of me. And I am much less of a pain in the ass! Most important, when my wife and I recently celebrated our 20th anniversary, she told me that the second 10 years were indeed much better than the first.

acknowledgments

I would like to thank several people without whose help I would never have been able to write this book. Thank you to James Carter, Rufus Dalton, Ellie Holt, and Kathy Sronce for comments on earlier drafts. Thank you to Karen Dalton for her comments and also for suggestions about content. Thank you to Raymond W. Novaco, Ph.D., for permission to reproduce his Provocation Inventory. Thank you to FBI Special Agent Patricia M. Parker for assistance with crime statistics. Thank you to Jo Sanders, Executive Director of the Chatham County (North Carolina) Family Violence and Rape Crisis Center, for assistance with domestic violence statistics. Thank you to Heidi Mougey for research assistance. Thanks to Paulle Chuchvara for her constant encouragement and to Dr. Jeanette Sarbo. A special thanks to Bruno and Cha Cha.

I am especially indebted to my editors. Marian Saffer ("Take the cuss words out, Tom.") was a constant source of encouragement from the beginning of the project through its completion. She was also instrumental in shaping the book and suggesting topics. When I was ready to bag it, Marian kept me writing, sending out proposals (which she also edited and helped to write, since we all know that angry men are terrible self-promoters!), and badgered me into continuing to work. Jill Metzler (the iron fist in the velvet glove) was responsible for many chapter ideas, for tightening up my runaway prose, and for helping me to "murder my darlings." Finally, Ellen Cavalli guided me down the home stretch and placed her subtle yet artistic (!) thumbprint on the final product. And finally, thanks to Shannon L. Donovan for saving me from myself with her copy editing.

To all of you, a humble thanks.

Tom Harbin
Chatham County, North Carolina
December 24, 1999

BEYOND
ANGER

PART ONE

are you angry?

1

AT THE BOILING POINT
anger's heavy toll on men and society

Why a book on *male* anger? Anger is anger, right? Yes, it is. But men tend to express their anger differently than women. Men are usually more violent than women. Men are generally less willing than women to confront and deal with their emotions. And as long men still hold much of the social and economic power in American society—which, right or wrong, they still seem to do—it's the men with anger problems who cause trouble for everyone else.

As a clinical psychologist specializing in the treatment of angry men, I've seen many of my patients lose jobs, wives, and opportunities because they were simply not able to handle the normal frustrations and disappointments in life. They argue, they insult, and they sulk. They come to think of themselves as ineffective, unlucky, or just plain losers. They don't admit this to anyone, but deep inside, they feel inferior. Others don't like them and they don't like themselves. Their anger gets in the way of their ability to be good bosses, good workers, and good family men.

I have also spent a great deal of time evaluating men who have been charged with serious crimes, such as assault and murder. Many, many of these crimes were not premeditated. These men did not all start out with the intention of hurting others. They reacted impulsively—often out of anger. Someone insulted them and they struck back. Situations that they could have walked away from became major confrontations because they did not know any way to handle themselves other than aggressively. They tell me that their behavior was stupid and that they don't know why they did what they did.

When I visit clients in jail or talk to men whose families have been demolished by their uncontrolled rage, it confirms my belief that society can no longer afford the costs of male anger. Domestic violence programs are deluged. Our prisons are overcrowded. Our courts are swamped. Marriages are failing as never before and single-parent households are on the rise. Even our schools are no longer safe. Certainly not all of this social burden is due solely to male anger, but much of it is: The vast majority of violent crime is committed by men, and irresponsible, undisciplined men desert their families and children more frequently than women do.

But you have a choice. You don't have to spend your life and your energy struggling in vain, hurting yourself or others with your anger and your inability to handle it. Instead of fighting against the world, you can redirect the struggle against your anger. No one can change the world enough to make all anger go away, but you can learn to deal with anger in different and more effective ways.

The struggle that angry men go through is often a lifelong process. There are periods of smooth sailing and times when nothing seems to go right. Sometimes you may think that you have finally overcome your obstacles, and then a setback will come along and you may feel the despair that says things will never get better. But as with most journeys, getting there is more important than being there.

You need to discover some new ways of looking at yourself. You need some new ideas for how to look at the world. You need to change some of your ways of dealing with the people in your life. And you need some suggestions about how to make all these changes. This book will give you those ideas and suggestions. Your situation is not hopeless—anyone can make changes in his life. The most important thing that will help you begin to move toward more peace and happiness is hope.

2

THE TROUBLE WITH ANGER
when an emotion becomes a state of mind

t's the middle of the night and you're sitting alone in the dark, just thinking. You've had another argument, you lost your temper, and this time you may have lost her for good. And you can't convince yourself anymore that it's all her fault. You said things that you didn't mean to say, and even though you wanted to apologize, you weren't able to make yourself do it. Even while you were yelling and calling her names, you wanted to stop. You wanted to admit that who was right or wrong wasn't important and that all you wanted was her happiness. But you weren't able to tell her. You weren't able to back away from a pointless argument. Why?

Because you are angry.

It's not that you *get* angry, it's that you *are* angry. There is a difference. Everyone gets angry from time to time, but you seem to be angry all the time. This is probably not the first time this has occurred to you—maybe you've even been told this before—but something has finally convinced you that it might be true. You may have had a big fight over a trivial issue, broken some furniture in an explosion of rage, or even physically assaulted and injured someone. Despite the defiant stance you always take, you don't really believe anymore that these arguments and explosions are always someone else's fault. You have begun to look more closely at yourself. You have begun to wonder if you have a problem with anger.

What Is Anger?

Anger is an emotion. And just like any other emotion, anger is not bad. Anger isn't good, either. Anger just *is*. Anger arises for specific and understandable reasons, just like any other emotions, such as happiness and sadness. Emotions are an essential part of being a human being, so if your goal is to completely eliminate anger from your life, forget it! First of all, this would be an impossible task. Second, you wouldn't want to do that, even if you could, any more than you would want to eliminate love, joy, or fear. All emotions have their proper place in a man's life; the experience of emotion is what makes life rich. And there are times when anger is an appropriate reaction to events and people.

Believe it or not, anger has its uses. It mobilizes people to action. It helps get things done. This is because *anger is energy*. When you get angry, you sometimes feel a tremendous rush of adrenaline. You get energized. You are less likely to feel pain. Your strength seems to increase. This potent energy can be used constructively, or it can be used to destructive ends. When things make you angry, you can choose to destroy the sources of your anger (and anything else that accidentally gets in your way), or you can use that energy to change your situation in a positive way.

It's easy to find examples of positive expressions of anger. Much of the progress in civil rights was made possible by the anger of the civil rights leaders and demonstrators. Much of the world's great art, music, and literature are expressions of anger. My own anger had many benefits. I was a fairly good athlete, and my anger allowed me to play sports with an intensity that I don't think that I would have had otherwise. In addition, I do not believe that I would have ever flourished at a major university and gone on to obtain a doctorate in psychology without the drive that my anger gave me.

The energy of anger *can* be put to good use. So, when you are taking stock of your own anger, you should avoid labeling it as good or bad, right or wrong. Instead, try to focus on the expression of anger and decide whether it is *adaptive* or *maladaptive*. Adaptive expressions of anger are constructive and help you to overcome the obstacles in your life. Adaptive expressions of anger do not harm people or property. Adaptive expressions of anger give people the energy and determination to accomplish their goals.

Maladaptive expressions of anger, in contrast, are out of control.

This type of anger energy ends up hurting people—and usually does not accomplish much. Maladaptive ways of expressing anger do not correct frustrating situations and generally leave you worse off than you were before. When you express your anger in hurtful ways, you are not in control of your behavior; you are being controlled by the frustrating situation that caused you to get so angry.

The Price of Anger

How much anger do you experience? While anger itself is neither good nor bad, having too much anger is bad. It's bad because it causes you or other people pain and because it prevents you from becoming a successful and happy person.

Research indicates that high levels of hostility lead to ulcers, heart disease, and other physical illnesses. Too much anger drives others away and leaves you alone. Too much anger ruins marriages, keeps you from advancing at work, and acts like a ball and chain, dragging you down and hindering your progress in most areas of life.

As you drive others away from you with your anger, you will eventually be alone. Fewer and fewer people will want to put up with you. Those nights in front of the TV can get awfully long after awhile without anyone to talk to. You can only spend so much time by yourself or so much time at work before you will admit that you are lonely and want more people in your life. Are you there yet?

Rage below the Surface

Many men find themselves unable to cope with even minor frustration. They get angry over trivial things, such as a broken pencil lead or an overcooked hamburger. Their anger erupts and gets out of control. They feel as though they are constantly under attack, that everyone is out to get them, and that nobody understands or cares about them. They may even get superstitious and believe that fate has it in for them, or that God has turned against them. This feeling of having no control leads to a state of continual frustration and anger.

This tendency to react with instant anger can be called *rage*. Rage is anger that never completely goes away. Unlike regular anger, it is not a response to a specific event; rather, it is a *response set,* or tendency. In other words, it is an automatic way of reacting to the world without much thought. When you react to more and more situations with anger, it becomes your habitual response. You may often find yourself furiously yelling or seething inside without even knowing what it was that made you so angry. Rage sees personal attack in every disagreement. Rage causes you to feel threatened when there is no threat. And rage causes you to viciously counter-attack even a minor threat.

Rage is like a wounded animal. It attacks anything that moves. And as with a wounded animal, the attacks do nothing to ease the pain. Rage depersonalizes individual people and events into a faceless, nameless "them."

"I'll show *them*."

"I'll get back at *them* someday."

Often, the raging man justifies his abuse of others as payback for all of the abuse (real or imagined) that he has endured. It is this non-specific, blind, and purposeless destruction that makes rage so dangerous. It is like a firestorm in its intensity and random violence.

There are degrees of rage, ranging from seemingly harmless to violently, criminally dangerous. Sarcasm and distrust are a long way from physical assault, though both may be examples of rage. Still, there is a difference between the anger that people feel when frustrated or humiliated and the constant, menacing, dangerous rage that lurks below the calm surface of many angry men. How, besides blind, unprovoked rage, can we explain the horrors we so often read about: the man who cruises the streets to find a vulnerable woman, who abducts her and beats her, who then rapes her and beats her some more? How can we explain unprovoked murder or gruesome mutilation? There is no threat to the man in these circumstances and there never was. While it is true that the perpetrators of such atrocities often suffer from serious psychopathological conditions, the blind brutality of their behavior is often driven by rage; this pathological rage is an extreme version of the tendency to react to the world of people as though they represent nothing but threat.

Of course, most angry men do not experience such extreme rage. But by the time a man becomes an angry man, he has probably developed a certain amount of rage. If you often feel angry and cannot say what you are angry about, that is rage. If you immediately assume the worst in yourself and others, that is rage. If you frequently lose your temper and strike out with little provocation, that is rage. If you often find yourself having violent daydreams, that is rage.

Rage can be controlled, but it does not diminish by itself. If you believe that you are dominated by rage, don't fool yourself into believing that you can change yourself simply by willpower. Your good intentions are powerless in the face of your rage. Angry men can keep themselves in check when things are going well, but the rage is always there, waiting to resurface when the least little thing goes wrong. You need help.

Anger's Red Flags

There are many warning signs of maladaptive expressions of anger. Some of these signs are obvious. If you get into physical fights or lose your temper and get fired from your job, it is clear that your anger was out of hand. If you find yourself explaining your aggressive behavior very often, you are angry. If you have broken furniture, hit your wife or girlfriend, or accidentally injured yourself in a moment of anger, your anger is dangerous and potentially out of control. If you have ever considered deliberately harming yourself, your anger needs immediate professional attention.

Other signs of maladaptive anger are not so obvious. "Road rage" is one of these signs. If you are prone to react to bad drivers by cursing, "flipping the bird," or driving aggressively to teach another driver a "lesson," you are angry. If your conversations usually turn into debates, you are angry. If you frequently use profanity, you are angry. If you usually see the worst in people, you are angry. If you don't get along with your family, have few or no close friends, and never seem to get invited out, you are probably angry. Other indications include excessive competitiveness in work or play, difficulty accepting criticism, difficulty adapting to change (especially in loved ones), perfectionism, difficulty relaxing, and, especially, difficulty acknowledging that viewpoints other than your own may be valid.

Anger can also express itself through physical symptoms, including a stiff neck, back pain, hypertension, and stomach and intestinal disease, such as ulcers or irritable bowel syndrome. Redford and Virginia Williams have discussed the connection between anger and disease in their book

Anger Kills. As they have documented so well, certain forms of anger, especially outward hostility, are important causes of heart disease. In fact, poorly managed anger ranks with high cholesterol and hypertension as a major cause of the vascular damage that leads to heart attacks. Not only does anger kill others, but it can kill you if you do not learn to deal with it more effectively. You might as well take a wire brush to the insides of your arteries as continue to damage them with your anger.

It is time to muster the courage to ask yourself some tough questions. It may be difficult for you to be honest with yourself about how you react to people. It is not easy to acknowledge that we are not perfect and that we make mistakes. But if you are not as happy as you think you would like to be, if you are hurting the ones you love, and if you feel like it's always you against the world, maybe you should relax your defenses a bit, and, in the privacy of your own thoughts, begin to consider that you may have a problem with anger

The Origins of Anger

If you are like a lot of men who struggle with anger, you are probably not sure what is normal, day-to-day interaction and what is abnormal anger. Maybe you aren't sure what "normal" is because you've never experienced it.

If you look at the families of angry men, you'll find that they often include fathers, grandfathers, uncles, and brothers who are angry, too. To a large degree, angry men have been conditioned to act this way by their families and society at large, and they simply do not realize that our behavior and feelings are not normal. They have never experienced anything else, and they assume that how they feel is how everyone feels.

If you were raised by an angry father, you have learned much of your behavior from him. If he tended to blow up with little provocation, you will tend to do the same thing. If he yelled and cursed when he was angry, you will tend to do so as well. Most unfortunately, if you watched him act with disrespect toward others, you will be prone to the same behavior. Most people convicted of domestic violence, child abuse, or other violent crimes were abused themselves as children and were witness to much more violence as well.

If your father was an angry man, chances are your mother was angry in her own way from dealing with your father. Similarly, if you have older brothers and sisters, they may have been full of their own anger. Thus, you may have been surrounded by anger ever since you were born. If you were never exposed to anything else, you would have no basis for knowing what is normal anger and what is too much anger.

Even if your home wasn't an especially angry environment, U.S. society does a lot to promote the ideals that can lead to anger. From the Puritan traditions of austerity, severity, and denial of pleasure to today's heavy emphasis on competition and humiliation of your "opponent" (whether in sports, business, or family), our culture sets men up for anger and unhappiness. Many religious traditions hold that denying yourself pleasure and comfort are pleasing to God. While I certainly cannot speak for God, I know that denial of pleasure contributes to many men's anger. And while you may find it exhilarating to humiliate your opponent on the basketball court, what do you think the effect is on him? How do you feel when a coworker trumpets your mistakes in front of everyone instead of quietly telling you personally?

Our society promotes an in-your-face attitude that is surely contributing to much male anger. In addition, we hear that more and more workers are working longer and longer hours and taking less and less time off. Since there is only so much time in a day, we must assume that we are relaxing and enjoying ourselves less. Take stock of your own life and decide if you have things in a healthy balance. If you are angry, chances are you do not have work and play, serious and silly, and intensity and relaxation working together in harmony.

Our admiration of pioneering independence and individualism has been good for opening new frontiers and exploring the unknown. Yet such individualism and reluctance to interact with others is not as beneficial for men's happiness. Isolation breeds suspicion and mistrust. Keeping yourself away from other people also keeps you away from the companionship and support that only other people can provide. Independence and self-sufficiency are good things. But cooperation and companionship are necessary as well. Virtually all people need other people. By acting as though this is not true for you, you are setting yourself up for a life of lonely anger.

Furthermore, striving to win and succeed is good for building businesses and reaching athletic accomplishment, but good sportsmanship and enjoyment of the game for its own sake have gotten lost along the way. In a famous pep talk, Coach Vince Lombardi told his Green Bay Packers,

"Winning is not the most important thing . . . it's the only thing." We men take winning—whether it be an argument, a game, a contract, or a place in the fast lane—so seriously that we often fail to see anything else.

Closely related to the feeling that we must always win—at almost any cost—is a fear of losing. Losing an argument, losing a bet, or losing a game all hit the angry man hard. It feels humiliating, so much so that he will almost never admit that he is wrong, even when he knows that he is. "Saving face" is an important concept in angry men's notions of masculinity. Angry men let arguments continue for days rather than apologize. They allow friendships to end rather than make the first move to resolve a disagreement. Such "pride," as it is called, is often a mask that covers the angry man's insecurities and need for the world to see him as flawless. This is an impossible and exhausting facade to maintain.

We should all take a hard look at our definitions of masculinity. Many angry men have themselves boxed in by a narrow definition of what it means to be a man. This definition usually excludes any tenderness, vulnerability, and flexibility. The emphasis is on aggression, intolerance, rigidity, and independence. Excluding such a large part of human emotion and behavior as unacceptable is like trying to build a house with only a hammer and a screwdriver. We also need to use saws, pliers, and levels. While the "strong, silent type" has been romanticized in movies with characters portrayed by such actors as Clint Eastwood and John Wayne, there is much more to masculinity than that. We pride ourselves on protecting our families, but emotional support is just as important. It is important to use more of the emotional tools in our toolboxes, tools such as empathy, patience, understanding, and the strength and confidence to let others see us as we really are. It is important for us to be able to comfort our friends and family when they need it, and we must learn to ask for help when we need it. We must develop the confidence to handle it when we are wrong, make a mistake, or get our feelings hurt. These characteristics are not incompatible with the strength that we admire so much.

Acknowledging Your Anger

To admit that your anger is a problem feels dangerous. You have probably avoided taking this step for most of your life, and it may feel as though you are going to be punished or humiliated. It took me years to cut through my own denial and acknowledge that I had too much anger and that I was not handling it well. Angry men deny their anger because admitting any imperfection makes us feel guilty. They avoid taking responsibility for their angry behavior because doing so means that they must take responsibility not only for its consequences but for changing it.

But if you want to change it, you have to acknowledge it.

If you are still not sure whether you are too angry, an objective measurement may be of help you. Dr. Raymond Novaco, at the University of California at Irvine, has been a pioneer in the study of anger and its treatment. He has developed a test to measure anger. Take some time now to take this test and find your score on the chart that follows.

Novaco Provocation Inventory

Instructions:

The items on the scale describe situations that are related to anger arousal. For each of the items, please rate the degree to which the incident described by the item would anger or provoke you by using the following scale:

1	2	3	4	5
very little	little	a moderate amount	much	very much

Use the same scale for each of the items. Try to imagine the incident actually happening to you, and then indicate the extent to which it would have made you angry by scoring the answer sheet.

In the actual situations, the degree of anger that you would experience certainly would depend on other factors that are not specified in the items (such as, what kind of day you were having, exactly who was involved in the situation, how the act occurred, etc.). This scale is concerned with your *general* reactions, and so the details of particular situations have been omitted. Please do your best to rate your responses in this general fashion.

1. You are waiting to be served at a restaurant. Fifteen minutes have gone by, and you still haven't even received a glass of water.
2. Being overcharged by a repairman who has you over a barrel.
3. Being singled out for correction, when the actions of others go unnoticed.
4. You are trying to rest or read, but there are children nearby who are making a lot of noise while playing.
5. Being called a liar.
6. You are in the midst of a dispute, and the other person calls you a "stupid jerk."
7. Hearing that a person has been deprived of his/her constitutional rights.

8. Someone borrows your car, consumes 1/3 of a tank of gas, and doesn't replace it or compensate you for it.
9. People who think that they are always right.
10. You unpack an appliance that you have just bought, plug it in, and discover that it doesn't work.
11. Struggling to carry four cups of coffee to your table at a cafeteria, someone bumps into you, spilling the coffee.
12. Getting your car stuck in the mud or snow.
13. You are typing a report, hurrying to make a deadline, and the typewriter jams.
14. Employers who take advantage of their employees' need for work by demanding more than they have a right to.
15. Watching someone bully another person who is physically smaller than he is.
16. Persons in authority who refuse to listen to your point of view.
17. You have hung up your clothes, but someone knocks them to the floor and fails to pick them up.
18. Being stood-up for a date.
19. Noise and disorder at the dinner table.
20. You are driving to pick up a friend at the airport and are forced to wait for a long freight train to pass.
21. You are driving along at 45 mph, and the guy behind you is right on your bumper.
22. You are talking to someone, and they don't answer you.
23. Hitting your finger with a hammer.
24. Newspapers slanting the news against persons in political office to make them look bad to the public.
25. You have made arrangements to go somewhere with a person, who backs off at the last minute and leaves you hanging.
26. Being joked about or teased.
27. Your car is stalled at a traffic light, and the guy behind you keeps blowing his horn.
28. Seeing somebody berate another person to excess.
29. Being pushed or shoved by someone in an argument.

30. You accidentally make the wrong kind of turn in a parking lot. As you get out of your car someone yells at you, "Where did you learn to drive?"
31. Someone who pretends to be something that he is not.
32. You walk out to the parking lot, and you discover that your car has been towed away by the police.
33. Working hard on a project and getting a poor evaluation.
34. Someone makes a mistake and blames it on you.
35. You get in your car to drive to work, and the car won't start.
36. Being hounded by a salesperson from the moment you walk into a store.
37. Being given an unnecessarily difficult exam when you need a good grade.
38. You are deprived of a promotion to which you are entitled because you haven't played up to the right people.
39. Someone tries to make you feel guilty.
40. You are trying to concentrate, but a person near you is tapping his foot.
41. Getting punched in the mouth.
42. When you are criticized in front of others for something that you have done.
43. You lend someone an important book or tool, and he fails to return it.
44. In the parking lot, the person whose car is next to yours swings open his door, chipping the paint from your car.
45. Getting cold soup or vegetables in a restaurant.
46. Someone who is always trying to get "one-up" on you.
47. You have had a busy day, and the person you live with starts to complain about how you forgot to do something that you agreed to do.
48. People who constantly brag about themselves.
49. Being thrown into a swimming pool with your clothes on.
50. Banging your shins against a piece of furniture.
51. You are trying to discuss something important with your mate or partner, who isn't giving you a chance to express your feeling.

52. Being forced to do something you don't want to do.
53. You are in a discussion with someone who persists in arguing about a topic he knows very little about.
54. Losing a game you wanted to win.
55. Being told to "go to hell."
56. Someone making fun of the clothes you are wearing.
57. Someone sticking his nose into an argument between you and someone else.
58. You are walking along on a rainy day, and a car drives past, splashing you with water from the street.
59. Acts of prejudice against a minority or ethnic group.
60. Someone spits at you.
61. You need to get somewhere quickly, but the car in front of you is going 25 mph in a 40-mph zone, and you can't pass.
62. Being talked about behind your back.
63. Stepping on a gob of chewing gum.
64. Hearing that a very wealthy person has paid zero income tax.
65. You have just cleaned up an area and organized the things in it, but someone comes along and messes it up.
66. Someone ripping off your automobile antenna.
67. You are involved in watching a TV program, and someone comes up and switches the channel.
68. Being told by an employer or teacher that you have done poor work.
69. You are in a ball game, and one of your opponents is unnecessarily rough.
70. Being mocked by a small group of people as you pass them.
71. Acts of economic exploitation whereby people in business make excessive profits by taking advantage of need and demand.
72. You are in a theater ticket line, and someone cuts in front of you.
73. Being forced to do something in a way that someone else thinks it should be done.
74. You use your last 20 cents to make a phone call, but you are disconnected before you finish dialing.

75. In a hurry to get somewhere, you tear a good pair of slacks on a sharp object.
76. Being misled and deceived by someone holding political office.
77. You are out for an evening with someone who indirectly conveys to you that you just don't measure up to his or her standards.
78. While washing your favorite cup, you drop it, and it breaks.
79. Children leaving their toys and play items scattered about the house on the floor and furniture.
80. Discovering you deliberately were sold defective merchandise.

Scoring Your Test

Now add up the scores that you gave yourself on each item. If your total score is 220 or below, you are doing pretty well and do not have a real problem with anger (if you have answered the questions honestly!). Scores between 220 and 280 indicate that you have a moderate, but significant, anger problem. If your score is above 280, your anger is a severe problem and you need to do something about it immediately.

Now you've got an "official" anger score to confirm what others have told you and what you have privately admitted. You are angry. If you are to become a happier person, something has got to change. In particular, you've got to alter the way you see yourself, other people, and the events in your daily life. Be honest with yourself. Stop automatically denying that there is a problem. Take a hard look at your life. Stop making excuses for your behavior. Your problems are not everyone else's fault, and just because your anger is not as bad as that of others does not mean that it isn't a problem.

Only you can decide that you are not as happy as you would like to be. Only you can decide to change the way you look at the world. Only you can make concrete changes in your behavior. You have to stop arguing over trivia. You must learn to listen to others, not just prepare your next rebuttal. You must learn better ways to handle frustration and disappointment. You must learn to be more flexible and accommodating.

These may seem like impossibly hard things to do, but I've seen it happen. I've seen men—including me—learn to relax, cool off, and control their anger and become happier people. The first step, as simple as it seems, is to recognize your anger—how it looks, how it feels, and how it affects everyone and everything in your life. The first step is always the hardest, but once you make the effort, you'll soon notice you're running full steam ahead.

3

THE MAN IN THE MIRROR
recognizing the many faces of anger

Things just don't seem right, do they? You can't quite put your finger on it, but you are not where you thought you'd be at this point in your life. One of my patients surprised me one day during therapy: He just broke down, seemingly out of nowhere. When I asked him what was going on, he replied that he had been thinking about what he wanted when he was a young man and how he hadn't gotten it. With tears of pain and rage exploding from his eyes, his angry regrets burst out of him.

"I never wanted much. A good job that I enjoyed. A wife that loved me. Children that respected me. A nice house. Nothing outrageous. But I've got nothing. I work my ass off, then come home to a wife who barely speaks to me anymore. And I've got a kid who's got a ring in his nose and thinks that all I'm good for is money. Where's my fucking American Dream?"

He drifted off into heavy sobs that seemed to lose anger as they gained despair. He repeated over and over to himself, "It wasn't supposed to be this way. It wasn't supposed to be this way."

If things don't seem right to you, you may want to ask yourself some questions about why you are not happier.

Why does it seem like I am always in a battle?
Other people don't seem to have as hard a time getting through their days as you do. No matter what you try to discuss with people, they

disagree with you every time you open your mouth—they question your facts, they argue with your reasoning. You get so weary of dealing with people as though they are the enemy; in fact, you feel so weary most of the time that you would just as soon go off and be by yourself.

Why do other people seem to be happier than I am?

Come to think of it, most other people seem to be happy most of the time. You look back over your own life and realize that, while of course there have been happy times, you are, at your core, not happy. Other people seem to enjoy being with each other, doing their work, going out with their girlfriends or families, happily living their lives. Things just don't seem to work that way for you.

Why do I feel so unappreciated?

No one recognizes how hard you work, how much you sacrifice for others. Your children don't respect you and don't appreciate all the things that you have given and done for them. Your boss does not acknowledge all the overtime that you put in or how your work makes him look good. Your wife does not seem to value the fact that you don't run around with other women, don't blow your money on boats or motorcycles like your friends, and spend your free time with her.

It may come as a surprise to you that your world view—the way you perceive life and the things you accept to be universally true—is quite a bit different than the perceptions and views of other people. For instance, you may believe that the world is like a hostile place where you can't let your guard down, even for a second, even among friends or family. Perhaps it has always seemed that the people you deal with are the ones who start the unpleasantness: your wife, your children, your coworkers. But here's something to consider. Maybe *you* are the source of the unpleasantness in your life. Maybe you are the one who is starting the arguments, who is turning every simple discussion into a disagreement. Maybe it is you who keeps everyone else tense and on guard. Maybe what you consider a normal reaction to given situation, or what you consider a reasonable response to criticism, isn't normal for other people. And maybe this negative perspective has a negative effect on everybody around you.

Many angry men don't even realize that they are angry. They have lived with their anger for so long that they don't regard their feelings as unusual. You may be one of those guys who doesn't quite believe that the way you feel and the way you behave differ from other people's emotions and behavior. Or maybe you have an honest desire to deal with your anger, but you are not certain what are and are not normal reactions to the world. You may need to develop the ability to observe your behavior more objectively. You may also need to become a better observer of other people.

In order to decide whether your anger is a problem, you must first learn what anger looks like. This may seem stupid to you—of course you know what anger looks like! Everyone knows what anger is. But there are many things about your behavior that you thought were "normal" that are not, things that you do that you don't even realize are expressions of anger. There are things that you do that everyone else does *not* do. Or maybe you take otherwise normal behaviors to extremes. For example, it's normal to become angry when someone cuts you off in traffic. It is not normal to chase the offender down the highway, looking for an opportunity to cut him off in return.

Take a look at some of the profiles below and see if you recognize yourself. You'll see that not all angry men are hostile, abusive, or offensive. Angry men are as different from each other in their expressions of anger as they are in their height, abilities, or favorite beer. Some men yell and curse when they become angry. Some silently plot revenge. Some pretend that nothing is wrong. Here is a partial list of some of the more common forms that male anger can take.

The Hostile Man and the Stuffer

Carl is the manager of a large manufacturing plant. He supervises a staff of over 200 people and is responsible for millions of dollars of equipment and more than a million dollars of sales each month. While Carl is considered honest and intelligent by his subordinates, he is also known to have a bad temper. If he has something to say, he doesn't care where he is or who is listening. If someone screws up, Carl chews him out. "God damn it, Dave," he explodes at one of his foremen. "I told you to get that machine back on line today. If it's not running by tomorrow, you can find yourself another job." Carl is yelling before he even discusses the problem. He

23

doesn't bother to find out why Dave doesn't have the machine running, even though Dave has always been one of his best foremen. He only knows that he is unhappy that his production is slowed and that this makes him angry. When he gets angry, he gets hostile. Carl insults, curses, and otherwise harasses those who make him angry.

Dave, on the other hand, says nothing. He has endured many of Carl's explosions and knows that "that's just the way Carl is." He feels as though he has no means or power to change the way Carl treats him. He feels as though he can't say anything or he'll lose his job. So time and time again, he stuffs down his anger and says nothing. He grits his teeth, clenches every muscle in his body, stares straight ahead, and endures yet another of Carl's tirades.

Carl, the Hostile Man, obviously has trouble handling even small frustrations. He goes from calm to furious in a matter of seconds, exploding before he gets the full picture of the situation. But his hostility does not usually make things better; in this case, Carl's embarrassed Dave with his angry outburst—and will probably not get his machine fixed any faster. Now, Carl is not stupid. He can see the way people look at him when he acts this way. He imagines that others think he is an "asshole." He is also smart enough about people to realize that those he treats so disrespectfully don't like it. So usually, when he has had a chance to cool off, he will go to the person he has cussed out and apologize to him. But no matter how many resolutions he makes to change, he slips back into the same pattern time after time. No matter how much he wishes he didn't feel so angry so often, he just can't seem to change. He feels helpless in dealing with his anger.

Meanwhile, Dave the Stuffer silently seethes in humiliation, frustration, and anger. Every time Carl cusses him out, his stomach burns just a little bit more. His neck gets stiff and sore, and he has trouble sleeping. The sympathy of Dave's coworkers only makes the shame and humiliation worse. Even though he knows that they feel for him, he wishes they weren't around to see Carl abusing him. In Dave's eyes, a real man would stand up to Carl, maybe even hit him in the mouth. He thinks of himself as a wimp. For hours or even days after such an incident, Dave replays the scene over and over in his mind, telling himself what he "should"have said and what he "should"have done to Carl. He fantasizes about beating Carl to a bloody pulp. And each time that Dave relives the scene, his anger is renewed, sometimes even intensified.

The Whiner

"I can't believe my stupid car wouldn't start again this morning. Nothing ever works for me."

Cliff is rushing by the other programmers in the office, trying to make up for the time he lost trying to get his car started.

"If they paid me what I'm worth around here instead of this chicken-shit salary, I might be able to afford a decent car. But the suits don't give a damn about the people doing the real work. They make more in a month for sitting on their asses than I make in a year."

Those within earshot roll their eyes at each other, silently saying, "Here we go again."

Cliff is a typical whiner. The whiner feels cheated. He feels as though he doesn't get what he deserves in life. When he looks around, it seems as though everyone else has a better life. Other people get more recognition for their accomplishments; the neighbors all drive better cars; other people have opportunities handed to them on a silver platter while he has to work and struggle for every last chance. He feels unappreciated, poorly rewarded, and unloved. He doesn't know how to make his life more enjoyable. Instead, he complains.

"Payroll? Why do I have to run the payroll program again? Doesn't anyone else ever have to do it? I hate this place."

Just as this last little bit of pleasantry pours out of Cliff's mouth, his boss walks by.

"Cliff, can I talk to you in my office, please?"

Cliff's boss informs him that Cliff's attitude is counter-productive and is contributing to poor morale. Cliff's fellow programmers have been asking for transfers, or at least different offices, so that they won't have to listen to Cliff's bitching all day long.

"Cliff, consider yourself on probation. Either you find a way to brighten your attitude in the next month, or I'll be letting you go. Your bad attitude is hurting the morale of everyone who has to work with you, and probably is hurting productivity as well. And that I will not put up with."

Cliff needs to get a grip. What's his problem? He is trying to get others to do things for him that he should be doing for himself. He is also trying to get others to boost his self-esteem. He whines so that others will reassure and comfort him. He has given up and become helpless. He does not try to fix the things that bother him—he doesn't look for a better job, he doesn't ask for a raise, he doesn't try to improve his work environment. He has no active hand in his own life. His passivity has become a habit and he has lost any ambition that he may have had once for fixing his unhappiness. And his constant complaining serves as a constant reminder of just how rotten his life is, thus continually feeding his anger.

The Debater

Eddie is very intelligent and witty. He is a great dinner guest who can be counted on to liven up the table talk. He is always good for a quick one-liner or comeback. He is very good in an argument and thinks quickly on his feet.

The underside to his quick wit is that Eddie's humor is often mean-spirited and embarrassing to other people. He will virtually never admit that he is wrong; for Eddie, there is right and there is wrong, and he must be right. When he cannot win an argument with facts, he resorts to personal attack and humiliation of his "opponent." He uses his wit to make a joke out of the other person's opinion.

Eddie's wife, Vickie, finds it difficult to talk to him about serious matters because the discussions always degenerate into debates. It is especially hard for Vickie to talk about her feelings with Eddie, because he insists upon knowing the "reasons"for her feelings. When she tries to tell Eddie why she feels the way she does, Eddie quickly shows her why her reasons for her feelings are "wrong,"and Vickie usually ends up feeling stupid. He will argue tirelessly every detail of the issue, and he can't let *anything* that Vickie says go unchallenged. He attacks her so quickly, so loudly, so coldly, and on so many issues at once that she has a hard time keeping all of his arguments straight in her mind. He continues until Vickie gives up, swallowing her own frustration.

Vickie has always wanted to have children. Eddie claims that he would like some children too, *someday*. One day at the dinner table, Vickie blurts out, "Eddie, I want to have a baby."

"Whoa, where did that come from?" Eddie replies.

"I just don't think we're ever going to get around to it and I want to have a baby."

"We've been over and over this, Vickie, and I'll tell you the same thing I always tell you. We can't afford a baby right now, but maybe in a few months we can."

"Eddie, I want a baby now."

Eddie starts sharpening his swords. "Are you on your period? You always get this way when you're on your period." This is his first debating maneuver—diversion.

"No, I'm not on my period, this has nothing to do with my period," says Vickie.

"Well, Vickie, why don't you think about my feelings once in awhile. You are always so focused on what you want. Do you ever think about anyone else?" Eddie's second maneuver is to make Vickie feel guilty for what she wants. "I bust my ass every day trying to give you a nice home and all you do is complain."

Vickie is once again in the position of arguing on several fronts (which are irrelevant) and not being able to get anywhere on her wish for children.

"I wasn't complaining," Vickie says, wearily.

"Sounds like it to me," says Eddie as he disappears behind the newspaper.

Eddie is trying to avoid his own feelings and keep the conversation under control so that it stays safely away from a topic that seems dangerous to him: in this case, his emotions. When Vickie feels sad or mad or otherwise unhappy, Eddie feels as though he is to blame for Vickie's unhappiness. In order to avoid this feeling of guilt, Eddie tries to convince Vickie that she doesn't really have any reason to feel the way she does.

He does the same thing to his co-workers, his relatives, and his friends. For Eddie, debating is a way to keep anyone else from "discovering" his true feelings. Deep inside, Eddie worries that other people are smarter than he is, make fewer mistakes than he does, and are generally better people than he is. Controlling the conversation prohibits anyone else from saying things that might embarrass Eddie or talking about things that he doesn't know much about.

The Abusive Man

Finally, we come to the most unfortunate of all types of angry men, those who are physically violent. While only a minority of angry men explode in physical violence, do not dismiss the possibility in yourself. Few of us know what we would do if we felt pushed beyond our limits. More important, do not decide that your anger is not a problem just because you have never been physically abusive.

Frank has been a fighter all of his life. When he was young, his father was proud of his aggressiveness, called him a "scrapper," and praised him when he "stood up for himself." As an adolescent, Frank was always involved in fights and often injured himself and others. He was confrontational and never backed down. He had an explosive temper. Now, as an adult, Frank comes up swinging over every little thing that goes wrong.

One day, Frank is working on his car and can't get a rusted bolt to loosen. He gets mad and jerks on the wrench. The wrench slips off the bolt, and Frank's hand is badly gashed on a sharp edge. He throws the wrench at the motor, breaking some wires. He then kicks at the wheel and dents the hubcap. So far, Frank's anger has caused him to injure himself and to do some expensive damage to his car. But the story continues. Frank goes into the house, holding his bloody hand. His wife, Christie, sees him and asks in shock, "Frank, what happened? Are you all right?"

"You stupid bitch!" Frank explodes. "Does it look like I'm all right?" As Christie reaches to help Frank, he backhands her in the face, catching her squarely on the cheekbone. Christie falls backwards, strikes her head on the refrigerator door and slumps to the floor, dazed.

While the Carls of the world attack others with verbal abuse and the Eddies put them off with their humor and debating, the Franks are consumed by rage and try to beat their way over and through anything and anybody that frustrates them. Their inability to handle frustration and their desperate attempts to stay in control lead them to brutality, sometimes before they even realize what they are doing. When Frank hurt himself while working on his car, a normal reaction, such as annoyance or temporary anger, was intensified by the rage inside of him. Without even thinking, he reacted to Christie's attempt to help him as though it was a deliberate insult. Frank's curses, insults, and violence will assure that he will become more and more alone and neglected, because everyone will be afraid to try to help him. It is also very likely that he will get himself into serious trouble. He may hit someone who is tougher (or more angry!) than he is and get beaten up. He may get sued. He may even be arrested for assault. If he cuts the wrong wire, breaks the wrong pipe, or slams the wrong door, he may injure himself seriously. That much uncontrolled energy is bound to wind up hurting Frank as much as it hurts others.

Frank has never learned how to deal with his own emotions. When he was a child, his father encouraged him to fight anyone who insulted Frank, teased him, picked on him, or offended him in any way.

"Are you going to let him talk to you that way?"

"You probably squat to piss."

For Frank and many angry men like him, the tendency to fight whenever anything upsets him results in an increasingly automatic link between unpleasant emotions and physical violence. Whenever Frank gets hurt, embarrassed, afraid, or jealous, he wants to hit someone. To Frank, his natural fear at seeing his injured hand, his natural desire to be taken care of, and of course, his physical pain are all feelings that are threatening because he never learned to cope with them. When his injury caused him to experience these feelings, Frank's inability to handle them produced even more anger.

Recognize Yourself?

It may take you a long time to recognize yourself in this chapter, especially if your own denial and avoidance are strong. Maybe none of the "faces"of anger fit you exactly. But don't necessarily decide that anger is not your problem because you did not see yourself described perfectly in this chapter. If *much* of it fits you, if you have *some* of the personality and behavioral characteristics described above, then you should be taking a good, hard look at making some changes.

What will happen if you ignore these tendencies? Clearly, abusive men like Frank will end up hurting themselves and others. But what about some of the other angry faces we met?

Carl, the hostile man, is going to end up with few friends. How long would anyone put up with that kind of verbal abuse if they didn't have to? What will happen to Carl if he explodes at a cop? Or at the judge when the cop takes him to court? And what effect will Carl's tirades have on his children and his wife? Hell, even the family dog is going to run and hide when he sees Carl coming.

Dave, the stuffer, may soon find it hard to stuff much more before he develops ulcers. He is likely to be so constantly and completely tired that he finds it impossible to do any of the things that he used to enjoy. He'll probably spend all of his free time on the couch in front of the TV, just trying to forget his life for awhile. His wife will start socializing without him, because he never feels like going out. His kids will play with the other dads in the neighborhood. He will continue feeling lonely, exhausted, and generally sick.

Eddie, the debater, is on track to lose his wife. She has the patience of a saint, but anyone eventually gets tired of being wrong all the time. No one wants to talk to him because they find it so exhausting. While he may have a potential career as a stand-up comedian or elected official, he will have to learn other ways of relating to people if he wants to have a normal personal life.

Cliff, the whiner, will achieve very little in life unless he learns to be more active and willing to take charge of his circumstances. He won't get the promotions that others get because he doesn't try to improve himself or his performance. He just complains when others get ahead. He is on track to be a loser, with a capital L. Soldiers in the Army have a useful piece of advice that Cliff could stand to heed: "Suck it up!" In other words, quit complaining and get the job done.

All of these angry men have damaged their personal lives. No one wants to be around them for very long. If you see yourself in these men, you may very well be on your way to loneliness, a dead-end job, legal trouble, or physical illness and injury.

And if you don't see yourself, read on. You may be surprised to find that the way you feel and the things you experience are right in line with the lives of other men who suffer from chronic anger.

4

WHAT ANGER THINKS
getting inside the mind of angry men

You have a pretty good idea now of what anger might look like. Maybe it looks like you. But how does anger *feel?* Again, you may be saying, "What moron doesn't know what anger feels like?" Remember, many men don't, in fact, know that what they are feeling is anger. Although they can say that they frequently feel "bad," they often cannot get more specific than that.

Let's take a close look at some of the thoughts or feelings angry men experience. You may be surprised to learn that some of the ways you're accustomed to feeling or thinking are very closely tied to your anger.

I Feel No Pain

Many of my violent patients report that when they get into a fight, they often go into a rage where they literally feel no pain. They continue fighting even though they may be seriously injured. This denial is a primitive protective strategy that many men use to deal with an unpleasant emotion, which is to simply not feel it. These men have a great capacity to numb themselves as a way of dealing with pain.

This numbing strategy works to mask feelings of vulnerability, fear, and abandonment as well. Angry men will stoically carry on when their wives leave them, their careers falter, or their hopes are dashed. Not only do they refuse to cry, but they also beat down any feelings that might bring out their soft sides. Numbing oneself, denying one's pain, *can* be effective in the short run; the unpleasant feelings subside temporarily. However, when particularly strong feelings or physical pain cut through this "anesthesia," the explosion of unfamiliar feelings can be truly overwhelming. Think of soldiers in combat who find themselves weeping or curling up in a fetal position, or husbands who find themselves suddenly crying or praying when their wives get seriously injured or ill. They can no longer ignore their emotions, and they feel helpless.

Angry men often see the ability to deny pain as a sign of strength. If you tend to deny your pain as a way of getting through your life, you may want to ask yourself which takes more courage and strength: to acknowledge the problems in your life and try to deal with them, or to pretend that they don't exist.

I Am in Control—Really!

No one likes the feeling of being out of control of his life. The sense of helplessness is frustrating and aggravating. Whether it is control of money, control of a conversation, or control of others, angry men rely on that upper hand to feel strong—and to hide any insecurities.

Angry men tend to especially prize self-control. For many of us, self-control strikes at the very core of our identity as men because our notion of manliness is so often limited to strength and independence. You may have a low opinion of men who "lose it," "spill their guts," or admit their faults or doubts; these guys are weak and "out of control."

Angry men also try to control the other people in their lives, as well as all interactions with others. They use control of conversation as a key strategy to control the events around them. It ensures that topics remain "safe." If angry men encounter anyone who cannot be dominated in conversation or otherwise controlled, they are likely to completely avoid future contact with that person. How many times have you tried to avoid socializing with people, using the excuse that you "don't have anything in common" with them? The real interpretation may be "I'm afraid that he will talk about things I don't know about" or "He's accomplished so much more than I have" or "He's better looking than I am." In essence, "I don't have anything in common with them" means "I feel inferior to them" or "I'm afraid of them." These feelings may cause you to avoid family members, your girlfriend's friends, or business acquaintances. Your insecurity and fear of humiliation lead to a constant struggle to maintain control.

Angry men make a particular effort to control their families. They demand immediate, unquestioning obedience in their children; leisure activities, friends, clothing, and hair length are all expected to conform exactly to their father's wishes. They expect their children to ask permission for trivial matters. Angry men expect their wives to submit their clothing, makeup, friends, activities, and opinions for approval. Another prominent way that angry men attempt to control their families is by controlling money. Very often, they have an obsessive concern about saving money. They won't permit themselves to spend or enjoy their hard-earned dollars, nor will they allow their wives or children anything but the necessities in life. Angry men often maintain a constant vigil over every penny that is spent. They scrutinize every purchase made by other family members, thus robbing them of much of the enjoyment of what they bought.

This intense desire to control is an attempt to maintain dignity in spite of low self-regard. Think about it. In addition to keeping everything safe, the exercise of power temporarily boosts angry men's low self-esteem.

"At least I'm the boss in my own house."

"A man's house is his castle" (implying that they want to feel like a king, with absolute control over everyone within the kingdom).

Like many kings and other powerful people, however, angry men will soon doubt the affection of those they control. They will always wonder if they are "really" loved by family members, or if their family is just acting that way out of fear.

What Did You Mean by That?

Angry men can be so oversensitive that they can almost never relax when they are around other people. They are hyper-alert to the things that others say and are always worried about the "real" meaning behind innocent comments that others make. This state of alert prevents angry men from enjoying where they are, what they are doing, and whom they are with.

Jim is a good example of an overly sensitive, angry man who sees insults everywhere. Although he forces himself to laugh when his friends are joking around, he cannot laugh at himself and barely maintains his relaxed facade when the jokes are occasionally aimed at him. He makes sure that he responds to any teasing with an immediate, half-joking counter-attack. Later, he broods about whether or not his friends were "really" joking or if they meant to embarrass him. He is also very concerned about others' opinions of him. At a party that he and his wife are hosting, someone remarks at how well his grass is growing. Jim takes this as a criticism of his "untended" yard and meticulously mows the grass the next day. Another day, when he and his wife are shopping for clothes, he picks out a tie that his wife doesn't think looks good on him; Jim feels embarrassed and assumes that his wife thinks he has bad taste in clothes—in fact, he obsesses about it until he has himself convinced that she thinks he is "stupid."

Hypersensitivity makes legitimate, well-intentioned criticism feel devastating for angry men. Any suggestions for improvement at work, tips on their golf swing, or even medical advice from their physicians causes these men to feel personally insulted and then angry. They need to be able to differentiate between disapproval of their *behavior* and disapproval of *them*. If you get angry with your doctors for suggesting changes in diet, angry at your boss for suggesting ways to improve at work, or angry with your wife for any suggestions about anything, you'll never benefit. Being overly sensitive can seriously interfere with your career, health, and personal life.

Not only is oversensitivity a cause of anger in many men, but the problem is often compounded by the fact that angry men tend to be selectively oversensitive. They are often only sensitive about the negative events in their lives. They magnify the significance of insults, humiliation, and failures. They dwell on, scrutinize, and replay the slip-ups, the disagreements, and the annoyances. They automatically anticipate anything that could possibly go wrong with a plan. They find the mistakes in a project and the missed spots in a freshly painted wall.

This automatic focus on the negative is accompanied by a tendency to minimize the positive. Angry men brush off compliments. They find any type of celebration, congratulations, award, or limelight embarrassing, so they avoid it. Angry men are embarrassed by attention of any kind, including positive attention. *Angry men seek out and emphasize the*

negative and avoid and de-emphasize the positive. With these twin tendencies, is it any wonder that so many men are so miserable?

Kevin has many talents and abilities. He is a hard worker (as are
many angry men), a natural athlete, and a good piano player. With all
of these abilities, Kevin has won much praise from others over his 50
years . . . and he has not enjoyed any of it. Kevin has avoided all of his
award banquets, has refused to be interviewed by reporters, and is embarrassed by compliments. He is never satisfied with his performance.
He is always quick to point out the things that he could have done better.
If he shoots a great round of golf, all he remembers is the bogey on the
seventh hole. If he gets a promotion at work, he faults himself for not
getting it sooner. Because he does not consider himself worthy of praise,
Kevin finds it difficult to take any praise seriously. He believes that most
people are being hypocritical when they praise him and don't really
mean what they are saying. He doubts the sincerity of compliments.
"She's just saying that to be polite," or, "If they really knew what happened, they wouldn't say those nice things."

You Just Can't Trust Anyone

Many of my patients are cynical and sarcastic. They are instantly suspicious of other people's motives. All officials are crooks. All bosses are exploitative. All compliments are hypocritical. Happy people are phony.
Anger leads men to see the worst in people. If all you see are people's
bad points, is it any surprise that you are unable to trust them or credit
them with worthy motives and aspirations?

This lack of trust makes the world seem like a hostile and dangerous
place. Many angry men act as though every personal encounter is
fraught with peril. For example, these men don't like to fill out applica-
tions for jobs, loans, or credit cards. "Why do they need to know this?
What does it have to do with this job?" They act as though no one can be
trusted in any circumstance. They lack the perspective that although
some people will take advantage of people *some* of the time, most people
and situations are not dangerous.

Without the ability to trust, angry men find it hard to make friends.
Some of them may have one or two good friends, but most people remain superficial acquaintances. It takes them years to allow a friendship

to develop from casual to intimate because they tend to reveal their thoughts and feelings much more slowly and because they are uncomfortable with others' feelings. Revealing your private feelings is the basis for close friendships; it shows the other person that you trust him and invites him to trust you. In addition to having difficulty making friends in the first place, angry men tend to place heavy demands on what friends they do make. They may be jealous if their friends have other friends, insulted if invitations are not reciprocated, or upset by even the good-natured teasing that friends do to each other. Consequently, they are often deeply hurt in these few friendships.

A different manifestation of this lack of trust goes back to denying or covering up our feelings. Do you have difficulty speaking candidly about most of your feelings? Is it because you don't feel that you can trust others with that much knowledge about you? When someone compliments you, do you wonder what they want from you? Do you become upset when your wife or girlfriend shares her worries or the funny things that happen to the two of you with her friends or family? Do you place great emphasis on keeping things "in the family"? If so, you have a problem with trust. Most people have someone that they can trust with their feelings—in fact, most people *need* this kind of intimate relationship. If you have no one, or only one person, with whom you feel comfortable discussing your pride, pain, or fear, you have a problem with trust.

How did this lack of trust come about? Maybe you learned as a child that no one can be trusted, especially with your emotions. Maybe your parents shamed you for your emotions, or used humiliation as a disciplinary technique. When an emotion such as fear has been met with shame (especially in a child), the two feelings can become paired with each other. So when fear is provoked later in life, shame is again elicited. In order to avoid the shame, other emotions are avoided as well.

When Louis was a child, his parents shamed him when he cried. He would wake up crying from a bad dream and they would admonish him for being a "baby."

"Big boys don't cry."

"Stop it or I'll give you something to cry about."

When he did have something to cry about—a skinned knee, a hard day at school, or rejection by a friend—Louis learned never to tell his parents. Now, later in life, whenever Louis is afraid, feels hurt, or wants to tell another person about something that is bothering him, he feels ashamed. To get rid of this unpleasant feeling, Louis ignores his hurt; he has become able to endure tremendous physical and emotional pain, but now he cannot get close to his wife or other people. When he contemplates expressing his emotions to them, he feels the shame all over again. Because Louis cannot express this important part of himself, the people in his life feel shut out, and both he and they feel lonely.

I'm about to Explode

Sometimes angry men's tendency to avoid expressing their emotions leads them to feel "bottled up." They want to say "I love you," but can't quite get the words out. They want to sympathize with others, but they're uncomfortable doing so. They want to express their unhappiness over small matters in a reasonable fashion, but they are afraid to.

The dangerous side of this tendency is that while such angry men feel as though many of their emotions are bottled up inside them, the one that feels the hardest to keep in the bottle is anger. Angry men often fear that their anger will explode out of control. Even though most angry men have never committed any major acts of violence, they are afraid that they will. Often, they can't be specific about what they fear they will do; they just fear some vague eruption of destruction.

"If I start getting into that, all hell will break loose."

"I'm afraid of what would happen if I told my dad about my anger at him."

If you try to get specific, you'll probably find that you wouldn't really do anything to your father, or to whoever bears the brunt of your anger. But it sure feels like you *might*.

The fear of uncontrolled violence combines with the overall fear of emotional expression to leave angry men virtually paralyzed for minutes at a time, unable to speak, with their emotions boiling inside. (And this paralysis makes them feel embarrassed, thus magnifying the anger and perpetuating the tendency to avoid emotion.)

As my patients approach the simple task of saying how they felt at a difficult time in their past, they often exhibit a common reaction. First, there is a long silence. Then, they come to the very point of moving their mouths to form the words, but they make no sound. Finally, they give up, silently shaking their heads and settling back in their chairs with a resigned and defeated sigh. It takes many hours of contact with a professional or good friend for these men to develop the trust that others are able to establish relatively quickly.

This feeling of being bottled up can be an actual physical feeling. It often starts with a knot in the belly and moves up into a constriction of the chest or throat. The closer it comes to the face and mouth, the greater the fear of loss of control. In some cases, actual anxiety attacks can occur. These involve dramatic changes in breathing and the heart rate, possibly accompanied by tingling and numbness that often make the person feel as though he is having a heart attack. For reasons not yet well understood, intense or prolonged anxiety can trigger a sequence of physiological changes that can feel as intense and frightening as a heart attack. The anxiety disturbs the body's normal regulation of blood gases and metabolic processes and provokes compensatory changes in the heart and lungs. These changes then drive the person's anxiety to increasingly higher levels, and the physical feelings become more and more uncomfortable.

If this has happened to you, be reassured: You are not having a heart attack, nor are you "going crazy." But you are getting a warning from your brain—"Wake up, buddy. Do something about your anxiety *before* you develop more serious psychological and physical problems."

It's My Way or the Highway

Angry men are uncomfortable with ambiguity, with the uncertainty that is characteristic of most real-life issues. Whether it's a favorite sports team, a political candidate or issue, or something as trivial as the color of a new tie, angry men often feel as though they cannot change their opinion, under any circumstances. To do so feels like an admission that they were wrong or stupid. They're rigid, and any disagreement with their rigid opinions by others feels like personal disapproval. They therefore find it particularly difficult to handle situations in which there is no "right" answer or deal with people who see the gray that exists for most issues.

This lack of flexibility also makes it difficult for angry men to feel comfortable in circumstances without clear rules and predictability: for example, in social situations. Most angry men don't care for parties, crowds, dancing, meeting new people, or any other situation that emphasizes spontaneity. For many of them, the world is a dangerous place, and it is very difficult to "loosen up" and relax their state of alert. It all goes back to the need for control—they avoid situations in which a lack of skill or competence might become apparent. Have you tried anything new (at least in public) since you were quite young? New activities are usually performed awkwardly at first, and you probably find it embarrassing to be less than perfect at anything. Angry men don't like to do anything that they are not good at. Spontaneity is a sign of self-confidence; there are very few spontaneous angry men.

I'm So Ashamed

Somewhere along the line, you may have come to believe several unfortunate (and mostly untrue) things about yourself, other people, and the world in general. You somehow learned that you don't deserve pleasure, that you have no right to be happy. Maybe your parents were overly shaming toward you; your teachers may have embarrassed you. Whatever the reasons, your capacity for joy has been mocked, slapped, insulted, humiliated, or raped almost entirely out of you. You may be deeply ashamed of yourself—ashamed of your imperfections. You may have developed a self-image of inferiority, incompetence, and ugliness (often both physical and psychological). Shame, like rage, is a response set. It's a constant, overriding feeling of guilt. People who are made to feel guilty too often or for no good reason develop a basic sense of shame. They develop an outlook on life that causes them to experience almost continual guilt.

Tony was raised by strict and rigid parents. They did not physically abuse Tony, but they used guilt as their main disciplinary tool. Tony was raised with the idea that he should always be productive, that leisure was sinful ("Idle hands are the devil's playground"), and that he should be ashamed whenever he wasn't "putting out 100 percent." As an adult, Tony cannot relax. He feels guilty if he is not productively active. The only vacations he ever takes are business trips. He has hobbies, but they are all "productive" (for example, refurbishing and reselling houses). Tony always reminds himself of the things that he "should" be doing. Tony not only has a hard time relaxing but also resents relaxation in others. He refers to his neighbor as "slack" whenever his neighbor is relaxing in the hammock while Tony is working around the yard.

The connection between guilt or shame and anger is immediate and direct. An immediate reaction to guilt is anger—in anyone. When we are made to feel guilty or humiliated, we feel devalued or demeaned, which leads to a feeling of anger. Think about the last time that someone deliberately embarrassed you in front of others. Immediately after you felt humiliated, did you feel angry? You bet you did. The same thing happens when you are made to feel guilty. Continual shame is constant fuel to the fire of anger. Not only do angry men experience shame from others, they are constantly making themselves feel guilty, thus preventing their anger from ever subsiding. This is not to say that all guilt is inappropriate— guilt is a method by which society and the individual maintain control over unacceptable behavior. However, too much guilt results in too much anger. If you get into the habit of feeling guilty (in other words, if you become chronically ashamed of yourself), the anger-producing cycle goes on continuously, hour after hour, day after miserable day.

I'm Worthless

As hard as angry men are on other people, they can be just as hard, if not harder, on themselves. Nothing they do is ever good enough. When you complete a carpentry job, do you only see the joints that don't meet perfectly, a detail that no one else would see? When you get an B+ in a course, are you disappointed and discouraged that you didn't get an A? Do you insult yourself when you make a mistake? If you answered "yes" to these questions, you are a big contributor to your own anger. It doesn't matter whether someone else treats you unfairly or you do it to yourself. It still gets in and affects you. Why is it that you only make remarks to yourself when you screw up? Why do you never say positive things to yourself? The things that you say and think about yourself *do* matter. And they contribute to your anger.

Angry men do not treat themselves well. If you treated other people the way you treat yourself, those people would have nothing to do with you. When you constantly beat yourself down, you become defeated and resentful. You don't expect others to treat you right because your life is full of ill treatment, much of it from yourself. You may tend to avoid responsibility or challenge because you expect to fail; then, of course, you get down on yourself for being a coward, for being afraid to take chances. You anticipate criticism for every little imperfection and for anything that might be construed as self-indulgence. You have come to believe, deep inside, that if people knew you the way you really are, they wouldn't like you. So, you deny yourself happiness, criticize yourself too much, insult yourself, and feed your anger day after day.

As you well know, angry men do not have happy lives. By breaking down the experience of anger into some of its component parts (like the guilty feelings, the difficulty expressing yourself, and the anxiety attacks), you may be better able to understand your unique experience of anger. While some things are true of almost all angry men, every man will express his anger differently and will have different reasons for his anger. You must learn to observe your anger objectively and carefully.

5

RELATING MAN TO MAN
the strong, silent type and roots of anger

Being angry all the time is hard enough on a guy. But if you have to deal with other people when you're angry, it's even more of a pain. If people would just leave you alone, everything would be fine, right? Well, unfortunately, you do have to deal with other people. You have to go to work, come home, go to the store, and drive on the freeway. All of this involves other people. In particular, this sometimes involves other men. Angry men are often not comfortable with other men. They become uneasy if another man gets too close, physically or emotionally. Why? Why do they find it so hard to let another man know who they are? If you are like most of the angry men I work with, you don't like to talk about yourself with other men. I don't mean that you won't talk *to* other men. You just don't talk about yourself in any meaningful way. Why is that? What is it about revealing yourself to another man that makes you so uncomfortable? Are you afraid that he will tease you? Are you afraid that he will think you're gay?

In my 12 years of treating men with anger problems, and in my own personal experience, I've found that men have strained relationships with other men and that many of the roots of men's anger can be found in these weird relationships. Yes, it's weird that many men try to avoid anything but the most superficial interactions with each other yet wish for something more substantial. For many of us, there are times when we need advice from another man, or maybe we just want to talk to someone about something we're going through. Many times during the first 10 years of my marriage, I knew that I was screwing things up and thought that it might be a good idea to talk to another man about it. I especially wondered what my father or another older man might be able to tell me. But I couldn't bring myself to talk to anyone about what was going on. Fifteen years later, I'm still not sure what held me back. Part of it was that I wanted to keep things private. But this wasn't the only reason. Maybe I didn't want another man to see that I didn't have all the answers, but that wasn't quite the whole reason either. I was angry with myself and sometimes with my wife, and I was confused about what was going on and why. But in the end, perhaps I just didn't have the confidence to trust another person, especially a man.

Men have a tendency to be contemptuous of other men for any expression of love, tenderness, sadness, or other "soft" emotions. They often look up to men who are tough, hard, able to handle themselves, and inclined to ignore their emotions and keep on going. This tendency begins in childhood, when they are ridiculed for being a crybaby, a sissy, or a "little girl." The teasing can continue into adolescence, when peers get after you for having girlfriends or getting upset. By young adulthood, the pattern is often well established and is exemplified by terms of contempt such as "whipped," "spilling your guts," and "breaking down." Anyone would react to teasing and contempt with anger. For angry men, it leads them to be careful to keep their emotions to themselves around other men.

Rules of the Game

A big part of why it's tough to connect with other guys is that interactions between men involve a whole set of unspoken rules. For example, you can shake hands, but you can't hold hands. You can put your arm around a man's shoulders from the side, but you can't hug him from the front. You can sleep two inches from another man in a tent, but never can you share the same bed. And, physical interaction aside, you can't admit to another man that you are emotionally affected by anything in your personal life.

I've seen this even in my office, a supposedly safe place where men can tell it to me like it really is. One time, a patient was beating around the bush, hesitantly telling me why he was "upset" at his wife. It was the end of one long day, and when I heard his whining, I lost a little bit of my therapeutic composure.

"Upset?" I hollered. "Your wife goes out partying with other men night after night and you're telling me that you're *upset?* How about pissed off?"

"OK, I'm pissed off."

"How about furious?"

"OK."

"How about you are so angry that you would like to beat her to a bloody pulp?"

Even though this man had been in therapy with me for many weeks, he still wanted to minimize the expression of his emotions. Like a lot of guys I work with, he prided himself on being able to suffer tremendous amounts of physical and psychological pain before admitting to another man that he hurt.

Not only are many angry men afraid of expressing their own feelings, but it makes them nervous when other men are emotionally expressive. They have many devices and defenses to help them to avoid other people's emotions. ("I just can't stand to see a grown man cry.")

One of these techniques is to keep conversations as short and superficial as possible. "How's it going?" doesn't usually mean, "How's it going?" when asked by angry men. They don't really want to know; in fact, they find it annoying if someone actually starts to say how it *is* going. Imagine how you would react if a guy at work responded with "Not too well. My father died last month and I'm pretty down about it." On hearing this and realizing that a friend wanted to talk about his feelings, most angry men would be uncomfortable. Most would find a way to get out of the situation with a superficial platitude. "That's too bad. But we all have to go sometime." At the same time, they would avoid eye contact and get the hell away from this dude.

Men even avoid potential displays of emotion by avoiding any situation that is focused on emotion. This goes for wakes, parties, farewells ("I hate good-byes"), even positive feelings. Have you ever been around a friend who has fallen in love and is rhapsodizing about his new girlfriend? Most guys will avoid the friend until he is able to "get a grip" on his emotions.

Have you ever noticed the men all standing around outside the funeral home during a wake? They are avoiding the emotions being expressed and exchanged inside. And what are they talking about? Not grief, relief, pain, or the exhaustion of the people involved (including themselves). Rather, they are likely to be gravely and seriously discussing emotionally "safe" topics, such as the patient's condition at the end, the particulars of the diagnosis, what the various doctors did and said, and so on. *Anything* but how people are feeling. They delude themselves that they have to be "strong" for their wives, mothers, children, or the surviving spouse, whereas, in fact, they would probably be of more use if they would show their grief and allow others to share their pain.

The Heat of Competition

This hesitance to talk about anything personal ties into yet another reason why men's relationships with each other are so strained and strange. From the time we are old enough to run, we are taught that we are supposed to be competitive. Not only are we supposed to compete, but we are also supposed to win. So why the hell would we ever admit that our relationships with our wives are faltering or that we have doubts about how to handle something personal? Life's a game, and the guy with the best wife, house, family, and job—in other words, with the best life—wins.

Men spend their whole lives trying to beat other men in whatever they are doing. I'm sure you've felt this. Whether you are an athlete, a lawyer in a courtroom, or just a guy having a discussion in a bar, there is always the pressure to win. A lot of men look for evidence of worth and goodness in their accomplishments. They define themselves by their successes and failures. Thus, they find it very painful to fail at anything.

When I was 16 (and already well established as an angry man!), I sustained a serious knee injury playing football. After having surgery and getting out of the hospital, I went through a fairly long period during which I just didn't want to be around other people. I was in a leg cast and walking on crutches and wasn't able to do many of the things that people do for themselves. Also, since I am tall and the leg cast was straight, it was difficult for me to get into and out of most cars. I hated being seen at less than my best and got inwardly furious when one day my friends tricked me into going out with them. If I couldn't be seen at my best, I didn't want to be seen at all.

When soldiers in the Vietnam War went out on patrol, someone had to walk ahead of the rest of the unit. These guys were said to be "walking point." This was one of the most dangerous jobs because the point man would be the first to encounter booby traps or snipers. It was a job that demanded intense concentration, great care about every body movement and noise, and more stress than most of us will ever face. One random move or lapse of attention and the point man and the rest of his patrol were likely to be dead. Angry competitive men act like they are always walking point. They rarely feel safe enough to relax. Do you feel as though "it's a jungle out there"? Is it "kill or be killed"? Do you believe that, because other men are out to beat you, you must continually be on your guard?

Here are some more unspoken rules for men: If you are not absolutely sure of what you are saying, keep quiet. If you are not a great golfer, stay off the course or try to play only with those who are worse than you. If your date is not drop-dead gorgeous, don't take her out in public. If you don't have a beautiful house, don't invite anyone over.

This continual vigilance is exhausting. It grinds you down and wears you out. Everything has to be kept in line, right and tight, and under control. Being constantly on the alert makes it virtually impossible for you to truly relax, drop your defenses, and enjoy the company of other men.

Is your reluctance to show your feelings to another man related to your ideas about strength? Do you believe that you are supposed to be able to "handle yourself" without help no matter what happens? Do you look down on other men who "spill their guts"? Does it feel risky to let another man know important things about you?

Well, showing your feelings to another man *does* involve some risk. Feelings involve vulnerability. Feelings are not perfectly controllable. Revealing your feelings means putting yourself in a position where someone would have knowledge about your weaknesses. You may get taken advantage of. You may get humiliated. But you may also find that a good friendship with another good man fills a need in your life that you didn't even realize was there.

Remember Eddie, the Debater? Well, he had always wanted to start a business of his own (so he "wouldn't have to report to anyone!"). After years of saving, he bought the necessary equipment and opened a shoe repair shop. It was difficult to build up his customer base and now, after two years, he is barely breaking even. Eddie's wife, Vickie, feels sorry for him and worries about their rapidly disappearing savings. She suggests that Eddie get some advice from a friend of theirs who has owned a local hardware store for many years. Eddie refuses, providing many "examples" of how their friend is no better businessman than Eddie is (remember, Eddie is a debater!). Vickie then suggests that he ask advice from the local chamber of commerce. Eddie replies, "Do you think I want those jerks knowing that I'm having trouble? How could I look any of them in the eye?"

Eddie can't stand for another man to see that he needs help, and he can't stand for Vickie to know that he is just as worried and scared as she is. So, he hides it all. Angry men hide their emotions even from themselves. "I don't care," "It doesn't matter to me," "No big deal," and "No problem" are phrases they use to convince themselves that they really are in control and don't need anyone's help. These phrases also help them remain unaffected by their emotions.

Emotional Vocabularies

By denying their emotions, by pushing them out of awareness, angry men think that they no longer experience them. But you can be sure that your emotions are still in you, and if you don't allow them to be expressed, they will find a way out on their own. They may get converted to anger and expressed in hostility. They may turn into ulcers, hypertension, or lower back pain. But they do not go away just because you refuse to express yourself.

Men's reluctance to express themselves emotionally leaves them with very poor emotional vocabularies. They don't have the range of emotion words that others have. If you want an example of this, take a piece of paper and list all the emotions that you have felt in the last month. Not thoughts, but emotions. ("I felt sad" is an expression of an emotion. "I felt *like* hitting someone" is a thought, not an emotion.) Then ask your friends, spouse, and parents to do the same thing. The difference between men and women in this simple exercise can be astounding. Women's lists are often long and detailed, including love, hate, happiness, sadness, joy, embarrassment, pride, concern, jealousy, devotion, satisfaction, and contentment. Men, on the other hand, will tend to have much shorter lists: "I felt good" and "I felt bad." Feelings that women would label love, pride, happiness, or satisfaction are lumped together as "good" by men. Similarly, embarrassment, disappointment, fear, nervousness, and concern are all labeled "bad."

When you don't have a vocabulary for a class of experiences, it is much more difficult to know how to handle those experiences. As an analogy, cabinetmakers have many words to describe wood. This reflects the importance of wood in a cabinetmaker's life, and it allows a cabinetmaker to describe wood with greater eloquence than other people. This extensive vocabulary allows cabinetmakers to articulate subtle differences in wood and requires them to experience wood at a more intimate level than other people. Similarly, the subtleties of one's emotional vocabulary influences the extent to which the person experiences emotion. An underdeveloped emotional vocabulary contributes to many men's emotional paralysis. Men don't like to talk about emotion, don't develop a vocabulary of emotion words and, therefore, are less able to experience and deal with emotion. In fact, it seems that the only emotions that many men, especially angry men, are willing to express are anger and lust.

The Missing Link

Part of the emotional handicap of angry men stems from the absence of mature men in their lives while they were growing up. When many angry men were boys, they didn't have men around to watch as they experienced sadness, grief, joy, excitement, or tenderness. Many never had the opportunity to see how men react to physical injury, praise, the birth of a child, or the death of a loved one. Many had no fathers in the home and no reliable men to fill in for the absentee fathers. In my work with accused felons, I have found that probably three out of four had no men in the home when they were growing up.

Even for those of us who had fathers in the home often did not have a man active in our lives. Many fathers believed that raising children was "women's work" and therefore stayed out of the picture; they felt that their only job was to bring home a paycheck. Others spent so much time at work that there was nothing left for the kids when they came home. Maybe they found their work more interesting and fulfilling than their home lives. Maybe they felt more confident about their work abilities than their parenting abilities. For whatever reason, even when they were there, they weren't really there. One friend of mine always wondered why his father had paid so little attention to him when he was growing up. Later on, in his middle age, he asked his father why. He had always thought that there was something about him that his father didn't like. His father admitted that he hadn't done much to be a loving father. "You know, son, I just didn't like kids." Strangely enough, my friend found this somewhat reassuring; at least his father didn't dislike him personally.

I grew up in an industrial city, and most of my friends' parents (and later on, my friends) worked in the automobile factories. I can remember my friend Oliver's father who worked in the "shops." For over 20 years, he ran the same machine on the assembly line. He could do the job in his sleep, and he hated it. The factory was hot and dirty and loud. The pace of the assembly line was fast, and Oliver's father was tired when he came home at the end of his shift. All he wanted when he got home was a beer and some peace and quiet. He had no desire to talk, to play, to help with homework, or to just hang out.

On the weekends, Oliver's father either worked overtime or camped in front of the television watching sports. Oliver virtually never spent time alone with his father. He learned how to play basketball at school. He learned how to ride his bike by himself. He learned about sex from other kids. When he was older, he learned about girls, shaving, working on cars, and fishing from someone other than his father.

As an adult, Oliver is quick to admit that he was never abused. He never wanted for any of life's basic necessities. There was always food on the table, clothes in the closet, and a roof over his head. But he went through a period of intense anger at his father. At first, he couldn't figure out why he was so angry, and he felt ashamed of how he felt toward his father. But then he started to realize that he was angry because of missed opportunities and because there was a big hole in his life that will never be filled. He never experienced the secure feeling of knowing that his father liked him and that his father would look out for him if things got to be too much for a young boy to handle. He was always on his own. He never knew the safe feeling of a strong male hand on his shoulder, of a strong male voice telling him that there was someone there to catch him if he should fall.

Today, Oliver feels like he has big holes in his personality. He feels damaged. He has never had children of his own because he always believed that he wouldn't be a good father. He did not have the confidence to try. Oliver realized early on that there was something wrong with him, and he felt strongly that his problems would get in the way of his own attempts to be a good father. By the time he figured things out and thought that maybe he could do the job, he felt that he was too old. Oliver now wishes he had children. He worries about being alone when he is old. He gets choked up when he watches other men enjoying time with their children.

Mother as Father

Women, especially mothers, have attempted to fill the void in their sons' lives. Oliver's mother often encouraged Oliver's father to spend more time with his son. She felt sorry for Oliver and tried to make up for his father's absence. She took him to basketball practice and went to most of his games. She comforted him when he got hurt. She tried to talk to him about girls. But women do not know firsthand about being a man. They can only provide a female perspective on what being a man is all about. What's more, their knowledge about what it means to be a man has often come from the same confused men that we have been talking about: their fathers, husbands, brothers, and boyfriends.

Women know what *they* want in a man. But this is not even close to a man teaching a boy what it means to be a man. A woman should not be the only source of instruction that a boy receives on how to be a man. Asking a boy to learn about being a man solely from a woman is like asking an electrician to teach someone about plumbing. The electrician knows quite a bit about plumbing because he works with plumbers, but there is a lot about plumbing that the electrician does not know.

Hollywood Knows Best

So, angry men don't learn about emotion from other men. Mothers are limited in the perspectives they can provide. Where else can men learn about emotion? From our popular culture. And what do men learn from our popular culture? Aggression, competition, and the virtues of sexual prowess.

Let's look at the movies. From Rudolph Valentino and Humphrey Bogart to Clint Eastwood, John Wayne, and Arnold Schwartzenegger, men are depicted as stoic, aggressive, sexually potent, and domineering. They kick ass and make women swoon! What other images of men are shown in the movies? Just the opposite. Wimps to be mocked and laughed at—the Barney Fifes and the characters portrayed by Stan Laurel and Woody Allen. They are sexually confused, inadequate goofball losers. In X-rated adult movies (which are generally produced by men for men), the pattern is repeated. Men are shown as domineering, aggressive, and able to bring any and all women to multiple orgasms of cosmic proportions. And while sexual relations between two women are frequently shown in these movies, homosexual sex between men is limited to movies produced expressly for other homosexual men, perhaps again illustrating the fact that our culture permits women to relate to each other on an emotional level that is quite different from the interactions allowed for men.

An aggressive and stoic image of men also permeates television. From the Westerns and war stories of the '50s and '60s to contemporary sitcoms, cop shows, and action shows, the two images of men persist: either the violent iceman or the bumbling, sterile sissy. There are a few exceptions to this pattern. But even today, when television depicts a less-than-macho character, he is hardly ever taken seriously: By the end of the show, the well-endowed female protagonist has usually made some joke about wanting a more "manly" man! In the main, the pattern persists, even in comic strips, advertising, and music.

This depiction of men as aggressive is not limited to movies and television. Many religious denominations adamantly teach that the man is the head of the household and the one who should direct everyone else in the family. Elementary and high schools still tend to steer boys into math, science, and sports and girls into English, humanities, and home economics. In the military, men do the combat and women do the support.

So angry men come into relationships with other men with one emotional arm tied behind their backs. They can't discuss their emotions, they feel the need to be in constant competition with other men, and they have difficulty trusting other men. All of these factors set angry men up to be isolated from other men and too many times forgo the help, support, and *fun* that other men can provide. They flounder along, raising generation after generation of angry men.

Problems of Principle

Many angry men feel as though they can never change their minds or compromise. To do so is to "back down" or lose face. How often have you refused to change your mind about something trivial because it was a "matter of principle"? That phrase is usually a smoke screen. Men might more accurately say, "I don't know how to back away from a confrontation, even a minor one. I would rather lose a friend than show any accommodation or flexibility. If I back off, I might as well admit that I'm a chicken."

This goes back to the personal insecurity that I discussed earlier. Angry men cannot stand to show any flaws to the world; they are not confident of their essential goodness, are overly dependent on the approval of others (although they would *never* admit it), and will do virtually anything to try to present an image of perfection to the world, especially to other men. In the minds of angry men, if they are not absolutely correct and righteous from the get-go, others will think badly of them.

Men, especially angry men, can't cut other men any slack. They are often rigidly judgmental with each other. With many angry men, all it takes is one small disagreement to permanently end a friendship. Many families have stories about Great Uncle Jonas and Great Uncle Ralph who haven't spoken to each other for 40 years. Why? Because of an argument over $10, or a flat tire, or something else equally trivial. How many people have you written off because of some unimportant disagreement? Do you have a good friend that you have avoided because of a stupid argument? Are you refusing to make the first move to patch things up? Many fistfights between men start out as minor disagreements that escalate because neither will give in on even a minor point.

You know the scene. Two men accidentally bump into each other in a crowded bar. One of them just *has* to say something unpleasant. The other, to save face, just has to say something unpleasant right back. Someone will then make a personally challenging statement ("Are you

the men's movement A recent cultural phenomenon has been the development of a "Men's Movement." This movement represents an attempt to recognize the pain and isolation of American men, to legitimize the "plight" of these men, and to propose male-oriented solutions for these troubles. The movement depicts men as isolated from each other by the demands of industrialization. The Industrial Revolution transformed the United States (and other nations) from a primarily agricultural economy centered upon small family farms and businesses to an economy based upon heavy industry, concentrated in cities. This transformation removed men from the home for eight to twelve hours every day for at least five days per week. As a result, according to the members of the movement, modern American men have grown up without the influence of their fathers, uncles, and grandfathers. More generally, we have not had the influence and help of mentors. We have had no one to teach us how to build things, fix things, interact with people, or handle life. Without mentors, men have a difficult time learning what it means to be a man.

To many uninformed, outside observers, of whom I am one, the men's movement seems to have started out with legitimate concerns and then gotten sidetracked. They have identified many of

calling me a liar?"), then it's off to the races. The men give each other no room to get out of the situation while saving face. Each feels the need to top the other's latest insult, and soon the fists are flying.

Ask yourself, Which takes more courage: to rigidly and inflexibly defend a principle, or to demonstrate a sense of perspective and willingness to compromise or walk away from a senseless argument? If courage is a worthy trait in a man, then accommodation, self-disclosure, and negotiation are more "manly" than stubborn rigidity, defending a principle, and privacy.

If you're tired of keeping up your guard all the time, if there are men around you who you think you would enjoy being friends with, if you think it's time to move on to a better relationship with your father or

the same issues that I and many others have been concerned about, issues such as emotional barrenness, confusion about the role of men in modern society, and relations between men and women and between men and other men. But somewhere along the way, the movement degenerated into yet more fuzzy-headed mush and New Age psychobabble. The adherents pick and choose this Native American ritual and that Zen tradition, without any apparent appreciation for the fact that the rituals fit within complicated cultural belief systems. Divorcing the rituals from these systems renders them as meaningless as it would be for a Christian to bow to the East and praise Allah every day.

The Men's Movement seems to me to substitute cheap emotional highs for realistic solutions for the things that men need fixed. Less time needs to be spent beating on drums in the woods and more trying to reduce the number of men who create children out of wedlock and then do not help raise them. Less time needs to be spent lamenting the difficulties that men face and more on accepting responsibility for change. Men do not need to offer their hugs as much as they need to offer each other their strong arms and their camaraderie. The Movement could do something valuable if its adherents concentrated more on substance and less on fluff.

brother, then what are you waiting for? The only thing that you accomplish by waiting is to let these distorted relationships get further hardened and locked into place. If you take the initiative, you may be surprised at the results.

6

LOVE, POWER, AND PAIN
anger and your relationships with women

One thing that pains and saddens many angry men—and is a big source of guilt—is the way that they have treated the women in their lives. From mothers to sisters to girl-friends and wives, the target of much male anger is women. A big reason for this is the imbalance of physical power between men and women. Throughout much of history, men have gotten their way because they are bigger and stronger and could beat their women into submission. Not only does such physical abuse continue, but the difference in power between the sexes has been institutionalized by politics, the workplace, and religious doctrine.

Another reason that women have been the focus of much male anger is because often, they put up with it. Regardless of your beliefs about the proper roles of men and women in American society, women tend to be more patient, enduring, and forgiving than men. Historically, they have not fought back, thus allowing men to perpetuate the system.

Other than trying to maintain the imbalance of power, why do so many angry men have such difficulty in their relationships with women? Men often find themselves in a situation that psychologists describe as an *approach-avoidance* conflict over women. An approach-avoidance conflict is when a person is drawn toward a situation because of the benefits but at the same time wishes to avoid the situation because of its unpleasant characteristics. A good example of an approach-avoidance conflict is deciding whether or not to accept a promotion. A person may wish to accept the promotion because it will mean a raise and greater prestige; at the same time, he may be hesitant to accept it because it will mean more work and greater responsibility.

Men are drawn to ("approach") relationships with women for many reasons. Like anyone else, they want a close relationship and someone to share their lives with. They may want to have children and raise a family. They may be attracted to a woman for physical and sexual reasons. They may find a particular woman intellectually stimulating and fun to be with. However, there are costs associated with any close relationship. This is where the avoidance side of the approach-avoidance conflict comes in. Remember, angry men have a hard time trusting other people. It may make an angry man uncomfortable when a woman gets to know him more and more deeply. While he is trying to keep the relationship within certain boundaries, the woman may be trying to move the relationship forward, toward more commitment, responsibility, sharing, and intellectual and emotional intimacy.

Other factors come into play on the avoidance side of the equation. Angry men find it hard to compromise, a necessary skill in any relationship. And while it is nice to have other people around when you want them, it can be annoying and frustrating to have them around when you want to be alone. When women in a relationship become dissatisfied and want to talk things out, men, especially angry men, often get uncomfortable. Many dread talking about anything personal, especially, *the relationship*. Angry men tend to see their wives' or girlfriends' desire to talk about problems in the relationship as criticism of them. They get defensive. The defensiveness then leads to one of two common reactions. The first is a hotheaded argument. When a woman does not agree with the angry man's side of the issue, he will often try to subdue her with hostility, shouting, and insults. The second response is the silent treatment. Many angry men find it frustrating to be disagreed with and will simply refuse to discuss the issue further. The silent treatment can go on for days.

A young woman recently returned to my office to try to find a way to deal with her angry husband. She had first consulted me several years ago before she married this man. At the time, they were having intense arguments over trivial issues. She desperately wanted to be married and ignored my advice to wait awhile and see if her fiancé learned to deal with his anger more effectively. Her fiancé attended one or two of the initial therapy sessions, laid out his good "reasons" for being angry with her, refused to discuss his behavior in the relationship, and never came back. Now, three years later, he is still too angry, she is still frustrated and heartbroken, and now they are married. She wants to have children but refuses to bring children into their lives while they are having such difficulty. And now he tells her that she is weak for seeking help with their problems—and he still refuses to come with her to therapy. Now, as then, he refuses to talk to her for days at a time when she does not give in to his verbal bullying.

Angry men often experience a great deal of conflict and confusion when they allow a woman into their lives. They tend to take to heart the old aphorism, "Women—you can't live with them and you can't live without them." Angry men, more so than others, don't tolerate uncertainty very well—they like things to be predictable and safe. And any relationship, especially between a man and a woman, is full of uncertainty. After all, a woman has needs that may differ from a man's and opinions that differ from his. She does not think or behave in the same way that he does, and he will not agree with everything that she says and does.

Uncertainty, compromise, disagreement, and intimacy can be frustrating and frightening to the angry man, potentially leading to yet more anger and problems in his relationship with a woman. Remember that when a person disagrees with an angry man, he sees it as a comment about his wrongness or badness. To compromise feels like admitting that he was wrong. Intimacy is scary because it leaves the angry man feeling vulnerable and his response to that feeling is anxiety and the fear of being humiliated and taken advantage of.

Control Issues

A primary issue between angry men and the women in their lives is control. Many angry men fear women (as they do most other people and most unfamiliar situations) because unpredictable people or situations may lead to exposure or humiliation. A lot of men do not know or understand women; I know I didn't. After all, women tend to think differently than men do; they have different values; their emotions are different. In short, they are unfamiliar, and therefore potentially threatening, to angry men.

The solution, unfortunately, for many angry men is to maintain rigid control, as they try to do with any other unfamiliar person or situation. Men used to joke (or maybe they weren't joking!) about their view of women with statements like the following:

"Barefoot, pregnant, and in the kitchen."

"Keep your biscuits in the oven and your buns in bed."

"No wife of mine is going to work."

But even though things have changed a bit in the past 30 years, men still go to great lengths to maintain control of women. Women are described as more "nurturing," thereby justifying an opinion that women should stay out of the workplace and home with the kids. There are still behind-the-back comments about not wanting a female boss, since she will be impossible to deal with "for four days every month." Similar justifications are used to try to keep women out of high public office, from the upper echelons of the military, and from the highest levels of most corporations.

If you are one of those men who try to get that feeling of security in your relationship with a woman by controlling her, your method will backfire. Because you try to "keep" your woman in this way, you will always have serious doubts that she stays with you because she wants to do so. You will tend to doubt her sincerity when she compliments you, has sex with you, or professes her love for you. Your own need to control will plant the seeds for your doubt and suspicion later on.

Angry men attempt to exert control over the women in their lives with various subtle and not-so-subtle maneuvers, some deliberate and premeditated, others automatic. For example, some men don't want their wives, girlfriends, or daughters to make themselves too attractive to other men. Think of the man who professes to dislike the way his wife or girlfriend looks with makeup on—"I like you just the way you are." Isn't it ironic, though, that the women he stares at in the mall, in *Playboy* magazine, or at a topless bar all seem to wear a great deal of makeup? What is probably closer to the truth is that the angry man is afraid that he will "lose his woman" to another man if she appears too attractive.

At the bottom of it all, this guy may be unsure of his own trustworthiness, his own attractiveness, and his own worth. This deep self-doubt can affect his relationship with his wife or girlfriend in a couple of ways. First, his negative opinions of himself lead him to assume the same negative qualities in other people. So he naturally assumes that his wife will be unfaithful to him and that other men will steal his wife if he is not constantly vigilant. He assumes the worst in his wife just as he does in himself and most other people. Second, he may assume that other people do not like him and don't find him to be attractive. This belief leads to the assumption that his girlfriend will leave him just as soon as someone more attractive or accomplished comes along.

If you don't believe that you are over-controlling with the women in your life, ask yourself the following questions:

• Who drives (controls) the car when you go out?
• Who controls the money?
• Who is not supposed to contradict whom in public?
• Who calls the shots during lovemaking?
• Who decides when the house needs to be painted?
• How would you like to work for a female boss?
• Have you had any extra-marital affairs?
• How would you react if you found out that your wife recently had sex with someone other than you?
• Have you ever used the following phrases in an argument or discussion? "Because I said so, that's why." "The topic is closed." "Because this is my house and what I say is the law in my house."

Let's visit Carl, the hostile man, again. Carl and his wife, Tracey, have been invited to a party, and Tracey would like for them to go. Their first disagreement occurs when Carl tells her that he would prefer not to attend.

"You know how I feel about small talk," he argues. "There's nothing I hate more than a bunch of stuffed shirts standing around talking about nothing. What a waste of time. What the hell do I have in common with any of those jerks?"

The truth is that conversation makes Carl uncomfortable, especially when he is talking to people that he doesn't know very well. He's not in control of the situation, and that makes him insecure. After all, he is used to being the boss, both at work and at home, where he has all the answers and can give orders and have them followed. When other people talk about things he knows nothing about, he feels stupid.

So Carl does not want to go to the party. Not only that, but he assumes that if he doesn't go, Tracey will also stay home. However, Tracey has already guessed that Carl doesn't want to go, so she suggests that she go by herself. Here's where the control comes in. Rather than let Tracey out of his sight at a social event, Carl grudgingly agrees to attend the party. But his cooperation comes at a price. Carl lets her know that he is doing her a big favor and makes her life unpleasant for the entire next week with his sulking and complaining.

On the day of the party, Carl is in an especially foul mood. When Tracey has finished dressing for the party—she is wearing a flattering, slightly sexy dress, jewelry, and makeup, and her hair is attractively fixed on top of her head—Carl takes one look and tells her that she is dressed like a "whore."

"So who are you trying to impress, huh?" he accuses her. "If I'd have known you were on the prowl tonight I would never have agreed to go. You look ridiculous."

They drive to the party in virtual silence. The only break comes when he announces that he is tired and doesn't want to stay out "all night." When they arrive at their host's house, Carl immediately gets a beer and stands around very stiffly, barely participating in any of the conversation or activities going on, and stares at Tracey the whole time. Tracey tries valiantly to include Carl in the conversations and introduces him to people she knows. Carl mumbles a couple of pained sentences, then retreats to his corner of the room.

During the evening, Tracey meets some new people, some of them men. All the while, her knowledge that Carl is angry makes her nervous. Around 10 o'clock, Carl suggests that they leave. Tracey protests that it is still early and asks if they can stay for a little longer.

"Fine. Tell me when we can go then," he orders.

"Well, I'd just like to stay a little longer and talk to these people," she says hesitantly.

"What *time?*" he growls.

They both reluctantly agree to stay until 11 o'clock. At precisely 11, Carl gets their coats, grasps Tracey by the arm, and firmly guides her toward the door. Once in the car, he is silent for about 10 minutes. Then he rasps through clenched teeth, "I hope you had fun making a fool of me."

"What are you talking about?" Tracey asks.

"Oh, come on, you ignored me all night. Not to mention all the guys you were flirting with—I saw all that, you know. Too bad I was there to ruin all your trampy fun!"

Carl's behavior is typical of controlling men who are chronically angry. If you see yourself in this scenario, you can be sure that your wife or girlfriend is miserable. Your stifling control over her is ruining your relationship. Your wife or girlfriend is suffering from her isolation and her constant efforts to appease you and to make you comfortable. She probably tries to keep the kids quiet when you are home. She probably tries to take care of household expenses without informing you because of your angry explosions. She probably dreads the times that the two of you socialize with others. And she is probably on her way to a good set of ulcers from constantly trying to anticipate the things that will set you off and deal with them before they come to your attention. In short, she feels dominated and controlled by your anger, and that is no way to have a happy relationship. Your tactics are sure to make her dislike you and wish that she had never gotten involved with you.

Sex and the Angry Man

You can bet that your angry ways are affecting your sex life. The angry men who visit my office frequently say they are dissatisfied with their sex lives, and their complaints tend to fall into some broad categories.

One common complaint regards the frequency (or infrequency) of sexual relations. If you think about it, it's easy to see how the angry man, by virtue of being angry, imposes a limit to how frequently his partner will want to have sex. Most of my patients say they prefer sex more often than their partners and feel rejected when their overtures are refused. This perceived rejection is humiliating. Humiliation translates into feelings of worthlessness and failure, which are then manifested as anger. And what woman is ever "in the mood" to have sex with an angry, humiliated, worthless-feeling man? An obvious cycle begins. The man criticizes his partner for her lack of interest, and his criticism makes her even less interested.

Too many of our egos are tightly bound up with a mythical ideal of sexual prowess. A "real" man is a sexual dynamo. He should be ready and able to prove himself anytime, anywhere. And real men are, of course, so good in bed that any woman craves his attention and has continual and earth-shaking orgasms. You probably know guys who refer to their penises as their "manhood" and any trouble with erections as "losing your manhood." Well, no man can possibly live up to this unrealistic standard. When their sexual experiences do not measure up to this exaggerated expectation, the men I meet with admit to feeling inferior and more angry. They routinely ask their partners about their "performance." ("How was it for you? Did you come?") If the answer is anything short of complete rapture, they feel like failures.

My patients tend to place an unusually heavy emphasis on their sex lives. I tell them that if they spent as much time thinking and worrying about their investments as they do about their sex lives, they would all be rich! Why such intense preoccupation with sex? For one thing, orgasm seems to be the most reliable way for a lot of angry men to achieve pleasure. If a man's life doesn't have much else in it that makes him happy, sex can be counted on for at least some amount of short-term pleasure.

Perhaps angry men are seeking gratification from sex that they are not getting from the rest of their lives. As we learned earlier, angry men usually are not happy at work, do not have many meaningful friendships, do not enjoy full social lives, and cannot take the usual personal risks that bring other people a sense of satisfaction. In other words, they do not get a normal amount of pleasure or satisfaction from other areas of life, so maybe they're trying to compensate for the emptiness that they feel by looking for substitute fulfillment in their sex lives.

"I've got a lousy job. I live in a dump. Nobody ever asks me to go shoot pool. *But at least I can have a good sex life.*"

This unrealistic expectation places a burden on the partners of angry men—a burden of guilt. The partners feel guilty that they are not "satisfying" their men, and all sexual expression becomes filled with tension. Nobody enjoys sex under those conditions.

When John was growing up, his father never told him anything about women. Neither did any other adult men. He learned most of what he knew about sex and about women from other boys his age, from pornography, and from television. Sex was something you "got" if you were lucky on a date and something that was mostly limited to the thrusting of a penis inside of a vagina. Shortly before John's wedding night, his father took him aside and had a "man to man" talk with him. He took John down to the bedroom and closed the door. There was a long pause while his father looked at him in a very serious way. Then John's father patted the bed and said, "Every day. Every day and your marriage will be a good one."

That was it. John did not feel comfortable asking any questions, nor did his father feel comfortable with the topic. If John had wanted to ask his father for more information, his father probably would not have known the answers and would not have been comfortable providing them. So, John does as his father recommended. He has sex with his wife every morning before they get out of bed. Because they have to hurry to get ready for work and because they have sex so often, they never take more than 5 or 10 minutes with each other. No wonder John's wife is not particularly fond of "it." She now views sex as something that she does for John, something to be avoided whenever possible. Of course, John senses this and believes that there is something wrong with him. Maybe he isn't attractive to his wife, he wonders. Maybe he isn't a good lover. But, of course, he is not able to ask her what's wrong, and her reluctance to have sex makes him angry.

Another common complaint my patients eventually share is that their partners never initiate sex. And this leads to a line of reasoning that goes like this: "She never comes to me for sex; she makes me do it all; this means that she doesn't like to have sex with me; and this means that there is something wrong with me or that I am unattractive or lousy in bed." I suggest to these guys that maybe their partners don't get the chance to initiate. These men are sometimes so insistent on intercourse two or three or seven times a week that perhaps the women never have a chance to develop the urge on their own. Also, by virtue of ignorance about women's sexuality (or just plain selfishness), my patients usually admit that they don't make much of an effort to find out what their partners enjoy and then try to share the pleasure. This lack of attention to their partners' wants and desires may make their wives or girlfriends understandably unenthusiastic about their sex lives. As the couple's sex life becomes increasingly filled with tension, both partners begin to withdraw from each other and avoid sex. The absence of a satisfying romantic life then leaves these men feeling lonely, cheated, frustrated, and ultimately more angry.

Violence against Women

Physical abuse is a complex phenomenon and several books have been devoted the subject. In Part Three of this book, I offer some guidance for learning how to control violent tendencies. Here, I address briefly why some men strike out and why their victims so often are the ones they love.

Not all men aggress in the same way or for the same reasons. For some men, physical abuse is a last-ditch attempt to gain control over a frustrating situation. The frustration may stem from the feeling of losing control, such as during an argument. The angry man and his wife or girlfriend get into an argument; if she doesn't back down, he gets more and more intense and frustrated and finally pushes or hits her. Or perhaps he is wrong and he knows that she knows that he is wrong, and he feels he has to win the argument by any means.

The amount of frustration that it takes to provoke aggression is different from man to man. Most angry men do not engage in any physical abuse at all. Others explode only under conditions of extreme frustration, anger, or provocation. Some men go from calm to abusive at the least provocation. In part, how quickly a man becomes violent depends upon the maturity of his tolerance for frustration and his coping skills. Some men can control themselves relatively well, tolerate frustration, and appropriately express their anger.

For most men, physical aggression usually represents a temporary loss of personal control. For others, it is a deliberate method of controlling others.

Vince lives with his girlfriend, Marianne, and her 10-year-old son, Sean. The relationship has always been difficult for both of them, and they argue frequently. Both Vince and Marianne use profanity when angry, call each other names, and deliberately humiliate each other during arguments. One Saturday, Vince is watching a football game on television while Marianne reads a book. "God damn it," Vince roars as his team fumbles the ball. At the same time, he slams his hand loudly down on the lamp table. Marianne looks up from her book and, in obvious annoyance, tells Vince to "chill out."

Vince is instantly on the offensive, asking her menacingly if she "has a problem."

"Yeah, I've got a problem with you cussing and knocking furniture around because of a stupid football game," Marianne answers.

Without taking his eyes from Marianne's, Vince reaches out and deliberately knocks the lamp over, breaking it on the floor. Shaking her head, Marianne gets up to leave the room.

"Where the hell are you going?" Vince demands.

"None of your business," Marianne replies.

Vince leaps up, grabs Marianne by the upper arms, pins her back to the wall, and sticks his face in hers. "I said where the hell do you think you're going?"

Marianne begins struggling to free her arms and inadvertently knocks Vince's glasses off. Vince slaps Marianne across the face, cutting her lip and bloodying her nose. Marianne spits some of the blood into Vince's face and Vince punches her in the stomach, knocking the wind out of her. At this point, Marianne's son comes out of his room, sees his mother bleeding and slumped against the wall, and begins hitting Vince on the back.

"Leave my mother alone," he cries.

Vince backhands Sean across the face, knocking him to the floor. On his way out of the house, Vince picks up one of Marianne's favorite family photographs and smashes it over his knee.

This episode depicts several important aspects of many incidents of physical abuse. First, there is a long-standing pattern of intense arguments, with deliberate insults. This constant undercurrent of hostility makes it more likely that a small provocation will result in physical violence. Some type of minor frustration enters the life of the angry man (here, the poor performance of Vince's favorite football team). His lack of good frustration-tolerance skills lead him to overreact to the frustrating event (cursing and hitting the table). The angry man's partner criticizes his behavior ("chill out"), which feels like a criticism of him as a person. He attempts to gain control of the situation by the implied use of violence ("You got a problem?"). If this tactic does not take charge of the situation, he then perceives loss of control, more criticism, and a feeling of personal rejection (Marianne criticizes Vince's behavior and attempts to leave the room). Finally, the angry man resorts to violence to regain control of the situation, and the violence escalates from grabbing to hitting until the woman is beaten into submission.

Once physical aggression occurs, it is very likely to be repeated unless some dramatic changes are made in the relationship. Past violence is the best predictor of future violence. In addition, intense arguing is very often a precursor of future physical aggression. If you frequently find yourself coming "close to the edge" with someone, you both need to make some changes immediately to prevent one of you from becoming physically aggressive.

In particular, couples who are thinking about getting married should reconsider if there has been a pattern of intense arguments. Consider this: A man in a dating relationship is on his best behavior. He is trying as hard as he can to make a positive impression. If he finds himself feeling so angry at times that he can barely control himself, he is not ready to get married. Once an angry man is married, he is less worried about making a positive impression. His self-restraint is reduced and he is more likely to aggress. Verbal and physical abuse before marriage almost always lead to more serious abuse after marriage.

In many American subcultures, men are subtly or overtly raised to believe that women need, want, and deserve to be physically assaulted. (The movie *Blue Velvet* comes to mind. And how many times did Cary Grant or Spencer Tracey turn Katherine Hepburn or some other starlet over his knee?) A myth persists that women admire men who slap them around.

"Women need to know who is the boss."

"Women are turned on by men who play rough."

"Power is the ultimate aphrodisiac."

Let's be clear about this. *Women do not like to be abused and disrespected.* Period. Abuse does not excite them sexually and does not make them admire you. Those rare women who do derive pleasure from pain have not had a normal sexual history. They have probably been sexually abused. If a woman often experiences sexual activity and arousal coupled with abuse and pain, you can bet she has become conditioned to the combination. In addition, if expressions of love are often coupled with physical aggression, a woman can begin to associate affection with aggression. But this is a psychologically abnormal condition and does not pertain to most women.

Of all the victims of men's anger, women have suffered the most. Their pain and indignity have been made worse by the fact that they have unwittingly and unwillingly participated in the development of the angry men who victimize them. By tolerating their own abuse, women contribute to the likelihood that they will be abused in the future. *However, this is not an excuse for physical abuse or justification of abusive behavior by men. Men are responsible for their own behavior. Angry men are responsible for the consequences of their aggressive behavior.*

These are confusing days for relationships between men and women. Even though women have not yet achieved equality with men in most areas of society, they are coming closer and closer. Men now find themselves competing with women as well as with other men. The old familiar sex roles are undergoing rapid change. You cannot relate to your wife the way your father did to your mother. Men will need to adjust to the new realities and to women with new ideas about themselves. You must learn to share power and responsibility with women. As you develop the ability to be more flexible and confident in your life, your interactions with women will become characterized more by sharing and mutual respect and less by domination and control. As you become more willing to consider other perspectives, your relations with women will become more intimate, more satisfying, less threatening, and less puzzling. You will be able to relax your vigilance and reduce the exhausting attempt to be in control of every aspect of your partner's life. What's more, what may now be your most frustrating relationship will become your most fulfilling, rewarding, and intimate one.

PART TWO

anger action plans

7

CHANGE FOR THE BETTER
the commitment to managing your anger

I f you have made it this far, you have accepted the fact that your anger may be excessive and that you need to do something about it. Believe it or not, you have already accomplished the most difficult part of becoming a more rational, more confident, and happier person. While you may not be ready to share your decision with other people, acknowledging your anger to yourself was a very difficult and courageous step for you to take. It means that you are ready to quit denying the problem and seek more effective and sophisticated methods for handling your unhappiness.

Let's get going. It's time to take your first steps toward a better life.

Step One: Tell It Like It Is

The very first thing you need to do is to quit denying that you have a problem with anger. Denial is a powerful defense for many angry men, but it prevents resolution of anger-producing problems. Denial protects men from guilt and humiliation because when they convince themselves that they don't have flaws or problems, they become impervious to potential criticism and other blows to their self-esteem. However, denial is not usually a very effective way of dealing with threats or other difficulties because it ignores reality. When you deny your problems, they never get dealt with. When you don't try to mend the problems in your relationships with family, friends, and coworkers, these relationships continue to go downhill. And since much of angry men's unhappiness has to do with personal relationships, denying problems means that men get no relief from their unhappiness.

Denial is a short-term solution that provides temporary comfort. Think of the athlete who uses pain-killing drugs in order to compete with a sprained ankle. He may be able to get through the game, but his pain returns as soon as the analgesic wears off. Not only that, his injury may actually get worse because he has ignored the important information that his pain provided. His pain is a signal that his body is damaged and that his ankle needs rest and protection. By continuing to subject that ankle to stress, the athlete has a good chance of worsening the sprain and causing himself even more serious injury.

Your emotional pain (anger, frustration, or unhappiness) is also a signal that something is injured. Denying that your problems exist allows you to go about your life. However, the problems don't get dealt with and may actually be getting worse.

At this point, it will be useful for you to admit several things to yourself:

"I have too much anger."

"I get angry too easily."

"When I get angry, I react too strongly."

"My anger is damaging my relationships with other people."

"My anger is making me unhappy."

"I am not happy."

For many men, acknowledging these problems will feel like admitting guilt. It is not. You are not admitting that you are bad, defective, guilty of doing something wrong, evil, weak, or out of control. Rather, you are acknowledging that you are human. There are no perfect humans, and we all have things about ourselves that could be improved. Don't be afraid to see the truth.

Step Two: Buy a New Hat

Once you have decided to quit denying your problems, you are ready to move on and make some changes. Make a sincere promise to yourself to give it your best shot. You may even want to make a public commitment to your wife, children, or friends and ask them to help you. What is most important, though, is that you get serious about this. The changes that you need to make will not be easy and will not just happen all by themselves. You have to be in command, and you have to put effort into making these changes.

Ah, yes, I hear what you're saying now!

"This is just the way I am."

"You can't teach an old dog new tricks."

"Why should I have to be the one to change?"

"It's not my fault that other people can't handle the truth."

"Other people should just accept me the way that I am."

How many times have you used these tired, old excuses? I can't tell you how long I let myself believe I couldn't change, and shouldn't have to. Don't let yourself get sidetracked by rationalizations. Remember, allowing yourself to change does not mean that there is anything wrong with you as a person. It is your behavior that is the focus. There are things that you are doing, thinking, and feeling that are making you unhappy. These *can* be changed.

You may be saying to yourself right now that you don't care what others think of you. But you and I both know that you really *do* care what others think. We all care what others think of us. Angry men in particular are very sensitive to what others think. Very often, it is fear of disapproval that causes them to avoid other people. It is fear of humiliation that prevents them from trying new things, from admitting that they don't know something and from allowing them to express the full range of their emotions. Take a deep breath and plunge into the process of change. *Only you can decide to change you, and you are the only one who can make your life happier.* Don't look back!

Many people find it helpful and satisfying to mark their intentions to change with some type of symbolic act. You may have some nasty, dirty, worn-out baseball hat that you have worn for years because you refuse to treat yourself to a hat that you would really like. Why not bury the old hat and start wearing a nice one? Burying has been a powerful ritual across time and cultures. We bury our dead. We bury important documents and cultural artifacts in "time capsules." We even "bury the hatchet" to put an end to arguments. Why not "bury" the old you? Why not make some changes in your appearance? Grow a beard. Get a tattoo.

Start wearing a tie to work. (Better yet, stop wearing a tie to work!) Consider doing something to mark the new you.

Take some time to think about your desire to be happier and less angry. Try to imagine what your life would be like if you didn't always feel so angry. You might even start to feel a little bit of hope that things can be better for you. Take pride in your determination to make some changes. The very fact that you have decided to do so is good. Most people would say that showing a desire to improve and better yourself is a positive trait. At the very least, make a bargain with yourself to try. No one can guarantee success, but all of us are able to make an effort. When you feel as though you have arrived at an agreement with yourself to make some changes, you will feel some peace. You may feel a sense of optimism. Don't dismiss it. Welcome it. *Allowing yourself to enjoy the positive feelings that are a part of every person is an important step on the road to happiness.*

Step Three: Fill the Vacuum

Once you've decided to try to become a happier person, you'll notice some changes almost immediately. The way you think affects the way you behave and the way you feel about yourself. When you decide to try to become less angry, you will begin to see not only the possibility of decreasing the angry behaviors but also of increasing the happy, contented, and relaxed behaviors.

Behavioral scientists have borrowed a truism from physics. While the physicists say that "nature hates a vacuum," it is also true that "behavior hates a vacuum." When you try to remove some behaviors from your life, you need to be ready with replacement behaviors. If you decide to quit working 60-hour weeks, give some forethought to what you will do with the extra 20 hours, even if it's only relaxing on the front porch. When you decide to quit beating yourself up about your "inadequacies," be ready with alternative, positive self-statements. If you decide to quit trying to control your wife's every move, find something to occupy yourself with so you don't dwell on what she may be doing every moment she's out of your sight.

Also be ready for the fact that when you change your behavior, several things may happen that will seem unpleasant. First, you will draw attention to yourself. People may notice that you are acting differently. Up to this point, you have probably tried to stay out of the spotlight because you don't like it when people notice you. However, the discomfort of being noticed will subside quickly if you can tough it out for a while. You have developed a fear of attention because you have assumed that other peoples' attention will be negative and humiliating. But if you take an objective view, you will see that most attention from others is not derogatory and is usually neutral or even pleasant. So, while the initial attention from your family, friends, and coworkers will be uncomfortable for you, it will not be as humiliating as it has always seemed. You have endured worse things in your life—like anger and unhappiness.

Here's a little tip: It may help to pretend that you don't even notice the attention. This type of pretending is a good way to change your behavior. Try picking out a friend, celebrity, or movie character that acts the way you would like to act. Then, when you are in a situation calling for new patterns of behavior, pretend that you are that person and handle the situation the way you think he would. *If you pretend to be a certain way for a long enough time, at some point, you won't be pretending anymore.*

Of course, the more major the change that you try to make, the more pressure you will encounter from those around you. You aren't the only one who has gotten used to your old habits. So have all of your family and acquaintances. Change is uncomfortable. When you change, everyone around you also has to change in order to accommodate the new you. They may resist the changes that you are trying to put into practice. For example, you may decide that you are now ready to accept party invitations, but your wife is reluctant. Give her time, and don't get unpleasant. Remember, she has had many bad experiences with you at parties. Similarly, your son may refuse your invitations to go fishing. Keep trying, and don't let the humiliation of a couple of rejections cause you to give up. People may even provoke you in an unconscious attempt to elicit your old style. When you refuse to lose your temper over issues that previously made you angry, don't be surprised if your friends continue to push the issue. They probably don't even realize what they are doing. Resistance to change is a natural human tendency. But if you persevere, people will adjust and accept your new style.

The process of change is like driving your car on an unplowed, snowy road. The ride is smooth as long as you stay in the ruts. Sometimes you can even let go of the steering wheel and the car will follow the ruts all by itself. But several things happen when you try to turn out of the ruts and onto a side street. At first, you turn your wheels, but nothing happens. Then the wheels find enough traction to leave the ruts. This can be uncomfortable as the car lurches over the uneven surface. Finally, the car settles into the new direction and the ride becomes smoother. Behavioral change is similar. At first, your efforts seem to be to no avail. You continue in your old, maladaptive habits. Then you begin to notice some change, and this is uncomfortable. Your life and relationships are temporarily disrupted. Finally, you settle into your new habits and life becomes more comfortable. Tough it out and persevere.

8

STOP PULLING YOUR TAIL
don't be your own worst enemy

Remember in *The Wizard of Oz* when the Cowardly Lion jumped and whined that "somebody pulled my tail"? The Scarecrow had to tell him that he was doing it to himself. Well, the same is true for many angry men. Much of the pain and suffering that angry men go through in their lives seems to them like it's coming from other people, but they are doing much of it to themselves. The next step toward becoming a happier person is to stop making your own life miserable. Stop pulling your own tail.

Angry men want to be treated fairly by other people. When they screw up, they don't want to be treated more harshly than others who make the same mistakes. When they accomplish something or do something good, they want the same rewards for their behavior that others get. In short, angry men expect the costs and benefits of their behavior to be similar to the costs and benefits received by others.

But do you apply these principles to yourself? Most of the angry men I know do not. Most angry men have much "higher standards" for themselves than they do for others. They expect more from themselves. They don't have any particularly rational reasons for these standards; if someone asked an angry man why he sets higher standards for himself, he would probably not be able to come up with anything better than "I don't know, I just do." What is probably true for all angry men is that their difficulties expressing emotions, uneasiness with accepting pleasure, and fear of humiliation have led them to treat themselves unfairly.

Be Rational and Fair

In order to begin to change the way you think (and therefore, how you feel), you must commit yourself to following two rules when thinking about yourself: Be *rational* and be *fair*.

As discussed earlier in the book, angry men tend to minimize and avoid any positive information about themselves. For example, they tend to "explain away" compliments. At the same time, they seek out and maximize the impact of any negative information about themselves. A good example of this is their tendency to brood about their mistakes. This is not rational. These twin tendencies to minimize the good and maximize the bad results in a distorted picture of themselves, other people, and the world in general.

In order to be rational, you have to think like a scientist. You can't hold any opinions about yourself or others without examining the evidence. You can't automatically take the negative to heart without objectively considering whether or not it is true.

One Sunday morning, I was fixing myself breakfast in the kitchen. As I took two eggs from the refrigerator and turned to put them on the counter, I dropped one of them on the floor.

"You jerk," I muttered under my breath.

I insulted myself automatically, without thinking about the truth of that statement. In fact, the evidence suggests that I am not a jerk. I have family and friends that love me. I do volunteer work. I am generous with my time and money. And I am considerate of others' feelings. So, a *rational* evaluation of the "data" suggests that I was incorrect in my characterization of myself as a jerk.

This may seem like a mundane and trivial example, so trivial as to be irrelevant to *real* anger. Calling yourself a jerk is no big deal, right? But imagine if someone else called you a jerk. It wouldn't seem trivial then, would it? It really doesn't matter to your emotions whether the insult comes from outside or inside. It still hurts and it still makes you angry. Now imagine how many times a day you say something like this to yourself, usually without even recognizing that you have done it. You probably do this tens if not hundreds of times a day. Imagine how you would feel if someone else followed you around all day and insulted you this often. It doesn't matter much to your emotions where the derogatory remark came from; it still adds to your negative feelings about yourself.

Be fair. Once you have obtained rational evidence for and against a particular self-statement, treat yourself the way you would your best friend. If you honestly believe that you've screwed up, then acknowledge the deficiency and get moving on a plan for change. Everybody makes mistakes. But most of the time you will find that your self-statements are overly harsh. So *be fair*. Acknowledge the error and resolve to confront and correct this statement every time you catch yourself making it.

When I called myself a jerk, I wasn't reacting solely to the fact that I dropped an egg. My reaction was the result of years of calling myself names, years of being embarrassed about any imperfection, and years of anger. If I were to have treated myself fairly, I would first have determined that dropping an egg doesn't make me a jerk—anyone can drop an egg. Then I would have fairly concluded that I am simply a human being who made a mistake and tell myself that I will be more careful next time I take an egg out of the refrigerator

Do Unto Yourself

A lot of angry men think of themselves as the type of people who would give others "the shirts off their backs." But what about asking others for help? A lot of angry men try to convince themselves that they don't need others' help because they are strong or proud, or they tell themselves that they don't want to "bother" other people with their troubles. Besides, they don't want to be in the position of owing anything to anybody.

In fact, most angry men don't ask for help because it makes them uncomfortable. It's embarrassing to show any vulnerability, lack of knowledge, or need for other people. If angry men do show vulnerability, someone may recognize that they have limitations, that they are not perfect. Well, here's a news flash. They do have limitations and *nobody* is perfect. It is irrational to deny or ignore this fact.

Angry men may also be uneasy asking for help because they are afraid that other people will think that they are self-centered or greedy. They may be afraid that they will be shamed for asking for something for themselves. So, out of fear of humiliation, they don't ask. Angry men are not being fair to themselves if they do not accept the same treatment for themselves that they would extend to others.

I have had several patients who refused to accept any help from anyone. I am thinking of Ray, who has always worked for everything he has gotten, has never accepted help from anyone, and has never bought anything on credit. While Ray doesn't owe anything to anyone, he also is not able to afford many of the things that others with his income routinely enjoy. Even though Ray would admit that the world had changed in the last 50 years and that credit is a necessary fact of life for many routine purchases (such as houses), he will not allow himself to change his behavior to fit the times. He lived in a mobile home for 15 years while he built his house, by himself, with money that he saved. Ray injured himself several times trying to lift things, cut timber, or do other jobs that require more than one person, all because he refused to ask for help. The whole time, and to this day, Ray has a much lower standard of living than his friends because of his refusal to be "beholden" to anyone.

You might think that Ray's independence and self-sufficiency would make him happy. But Ray was not a happy man when I met him. In fact, Ray became furious with me when I did not seem to admire his independence. I had asked him a simple question: "What has all of your independence done to make you happy?" He replied that he was "proud" to be self-sufficient. I persisted, "But are you *happy*?" That was a question he wasn't prepared to answer.

Rather than protect him from embarrassment, Ray's refusal to accept help actually has made him more embarrassed. He doesn't have the same comforts in life that the rest of the neighbors do, and this makes Ray feel like a failure. He works 10 to 30 hours more per week than other men and has less to show for it. This has contributed to his anger, bitterness, and cynicism. He refuses to be around the other guys in the neighborhood, whom he describes as "show-offs." He never accepts invitations to go fishing because he is embarrassed that his friends have boats and he doesn't. He won't go to parties because he is uncomfortable around other people, especially people who are laughing and acting happy. As a result, people have stopped inviting Ray to participate in their fun, and he has become isolated.

My patient had violated our first principle of fairness. He was not treating himself in the same way as he would treat others. He would give help but never accept help. Not only help, but pleasure—Ray would never slow down to laugh, relax, goof off, take vacations, dance, accept presents, or even buy himself some good beer every now and then. Is it any wonder that he was angry?

fairness exercise: say yes!

You have to start treating yourself the way you would treat other people. Otherwise, you will never be happy. And you will continue to be angry as long you refuse to let yourself be happy. You must curb your impulse to say "no" all the time. This will be a difficult change to make because "no" has become an almost automatic response by now. You probably react to most invitations, impulses, or change with suspicion and avoidance. Take a chance. Let yourself experience some of the things that other people seem to enjoy. You won't like all of it. But if you give yourself a chance, you will like some of it.

Try this: At least once a week for a month, agree to something that you would normally say "no" to. Accept an invitation. Volunteer for an interesting project at work. Ask a friend to help with a home improvement task. Do something out of the ordinary. It won't always be fun, but sometimes it will. You might also try this: When someone asks you to do something fun or if you consider doing something yourself, don't answer right away. Go off somewhere private and make a list the pros and cons. Chances are that most of the time there won't be any good reasons to say "no."

Let the Punishment Fit the Crime

When someone screws up and does something wrong, most of us expect that whatever punishment the person gets should fit the "crime" that he committed. In other words, a misdemeanor should be treated less harshly than a felony. Similarly, we expect our rewards to be in proportion to our accomplishments. We don't expect a $1,000 bonus for getting to work on time every day, but we do expect to be acknowledged and rewarded when we accomplish something major.

But angry men don't usually treat themselves in accordance with these principles. When they make a mistake or do something they

Penance exercise: does it really matter?

This is an exercise that I assign to many of my angry patients, and you should give it a try.

First, when you are getting down on yourself for something that you have done (you may even still be feeling guilty for minor events in your childhood), take a minute to consider how important the screw-up is *now*. (At this point, my patients will try to tell me how badly they treated someone or how big of a mistake they made. But I persist.) How much difference does it make to anyone *now*? The answer is probably that it doesn't make much difference now, right?

The next step is to decide if your time would be better spent continuing to fret over this past incident or working on improving for the future. I suggest that you need a "mantra" to help you do this. If you are old enough to remember the 1960s, you may remember that meditation was very popular. Many forms of meditation encourage the chanting of a simple word over and over again to clear the mind and sharpen one's focus. "Ommmmmm" was a popular chant. In this case, I suggest chanting "Let it go" or "It doesn't matter" or "I don't care." These "mantras" will remind you to ease up, but they can also be relaxing in their own right.

shouldn't have done, they tend to feel overly guilty. They are too harsh on themselves. They do not punish themselves in proportion to their crimes.

James has been under a lot of pressure at work in the past several weeks. He is in charge of his company's display at a large trade show; the show is a week away and there are the usual problems and last-minute details to take care of. One of his workers asks James if the company's catalogs have been put on the truck going to the show. James replies with some irritation, "Go check for yourself. You know where the truck is. Do I have to do everything myself?"

By the look on his helper's face, James knows that he has hurt his feelings. James immediately feels terribly guilty. His mind begins to replay the scene over and over again, each time magnifying the seriousness of what he has done. He continues to feel guilty the next day and the next. He comes to the point where he believes that his helper will never respect him again, and that furthermore, he is a lousy manager for speaking to one of his men that way. Finally, James feels compelled to apologize.

"Joe, I'm really sorry for grouching at you the other day. It's bothered me all week and I wanted to apologize to you."

"What are you talking about, James?" replies Joe.

Puzzled, James says, "You know, last week, when you asked me about the catalogs."

"Oh, that," laughs Joe. "Forget it. You had a rough day and I should have checked for the stuff myself. Don't worry about it."

James is relieved that Joe isn't mad at him. But he is also puzzled and confused. He thought that he had been seriously out of line and further believed that Joe probably thought he was an asshole.

The point is that James had magnified the intensity of his actions well beyond their importance to Joe. He punished himself for a week over something that Joe got over quickly. James does this all the time. He always dwells on his faults, failures, and imperfections to the point where he almost always feels the need to do "penance."

Take Happiness Like a Man

There's more than one way to pull your own tail. A lot of angry men contribute to their anger by "punishing" themselves more frequently and more intensely than they deserve. Unfortunately, this tendency to be too hard on themselves is often accompanied by a reluctance to accept the good things in life. So, with one hand, angry men are piling misery on themselves, and with the other, they are holding all the good stuff away. This sounds crazy, doesn't it?

Why do angry men deny themselves pleasure? For many of them, this tendency arises from a deep sense of personal inferiority. If you recall from Chapter 4, many angry men just do not believe that they are as good as other people. They don't believe that they deserve praise or even happiness. They believe that they are not as accomplished, as handsome,

Happiness exercise: ask and receive?

Ask someone for help or for their opinion—even if you don't need it—at least once a week. In addition, from now on, for the rest of your life, when someone gives you a compliment, allow yourself only to say "Thank you."

witty, successful, honest, caring, thoughtful, or charming as others. And angry men are afraid that someone will find out just how inferior they are. This core belief of inferiority prevents angry men from enjoying acknowledgment or praise. Remember Kevin, who we met in Chapter 4? He wouldn't even attend awards banquets in his honor because he felt like a hypocrite. "If they really knew what I'm like, they wouldn't be so nice to me."

When angry men then project their own feelings of hypocrisy onto others, they come to believe that all compliments are insincere. Because they really don't trust anyone, they believe that any nice treatment by others is something to be wary of. Most men who fall into this trap do not even realize that they think this way about themselves. When asked why they don't enjoy compliments, angry men usually cannot give a good explanation. They just know that the positive attention makes them uncomfortable.

These two beliefs by angry men, that they do not deserve to be happy and that others think badly of them, keep them constantly on guard. Angry men always watch themselves to make sure that no flaw is evident, that they don't say the wrong thing, appear ignorant, or need help. This wariness is exhausting. Never letting your guard down is like being in a boxing match with no breaks between rounds. One of the hardest things for a boxer to do when he is getting tired in the later rounds is to keep his hands up (his guard). At least the boxer gets a break between rounds and is able to rest his guard. Angry men seldom if ever get a rest. Keeping their guard up drains energy and reduces even further their ability to handle stress and frustration, making it even more likely that they will get angry.

Recognize Your Irrational Thoughts

Now we come to what is probably the most important thing that angry men can do to make life happier. I have been talking about maladaptive or distorted thinking throughout this book, and I have been implying that, sooner or later, this maladaptive thinking is going to have to change. So, here we go.

The first step in correcting your distorted, irrational, maladaptive thinking is to learn to recognize it when you are experiencing it. This seems like a simple proposition, but it is difficult to put into practice. Most angry men are not used to examining the thoughts behind their emotions; they just feel the emotions. But when anger strikes, you must begin to ask yourself, "Why?" In order to do this, you have to learn to step out of the anger-producing situations that you find yourself in and observe yourself as though you were a neutral third party.

The next thing that you have to learn to do is to review the sequence of events that happened when you got angry. You have to pay attention to what everyone said, what you thought at each step of the process, and how your emotions changed throughout the event. A typical sequence might go as follows.

Let's say you come home from work tired and angry (as usual!). Your wife greets you as you come in the door and asks you how your day was. You find this question irritating and mumble something like "the usual" or "same shit, different day." Your wife continues to try to make conversation and asks you, "Did anything exciting happen?" For some reason, this really pisses you off and you snap, "I told you it was just another day." You have set the tone for another tense, silent, and uncomfortable evening. Why? What made you so angry so quickly?

An obvious conclusion is that it wasn't anything that your wife said at that moment that made you angry. You were irritable when you got home. An angry response is usually more than a response to the immediate incident: anger is influenced by the remote past, the immediate past, and whatever is going on right at this instant. This is important. *Very often, the immediate event that leads to anger is not the real cause of the anger.* Maybe you are so exhausted from trying to deal with people all day that you just want to be left alone. Maybe *any* question from *anyone* feels like an intrusion or a threat to you right now.

But let's examine the immediate scene a bit more closely. All your wife did was ask you how your day went, and you found this annoying. Why? Maybe you don't think that she is sincerely interested in your day, since she asks you every day. If you don't believe that she is sincere, this indicates that you doesn't trust her to be honest. If you believe that your wife's question about your day is not sincere, you might really be saying to yourself, "She doesn't really care how my day went." And if she doesn't care how your day went, you determine that "She doesn't really care about me." This, in turn, leads to, "There is something wrong with me," "I'm bad," or some version of that theme. The sequence of thoughts you put yourself through usually gets more and more personal until you arrive at some negative statement about yourself personally.

Maybe you're not aware that you make statements like this to yourself. For angry men especially, these self-statements happen so often that they become automatic. *Any* criticism, *any* questioning of opinion, *any* loss of control instantly leads to a feeling of worthlessness. And both the good and the bad news is, *you're doing it to yourself*—bad news because self-inflicted pain is preventable, good news because you have the potential to eliminate this pain from your life. You are pulling your own tail.

I know it's hard to believe this sequence of events, especially the end point ("I'm bad"). But remember that we all will have different things that we say to ourselves. For example, it is unlikely that anyone actually says, "I'm bad." But it is not so hard to believe that you might think that something must be wrong with you, since everyone seems to be so disrespectful toward you. Also remember that these thoughts become so automatic and happen so quickly that you have to concentrate and practice at first in order to be aware of them. But in order to get a handle on your anger, you must begin to recognize these automatic self-statements.

You will be surprised at how frequently you are making such statements to yourself about yourself. It will seem as though you are continually engaging in this distorted style of thinking. Don't be discouraged. By writing all of this stuff down, you are developing insight into your emotions, especially your anger. And there is an added bonus: Even though we have not yet described methods for changing these thought patterns, many of my patients find that the simple act of analyzing their emotions in this way helps them to make some changes on their own, without any further help.

The bottom line is, you deserve to be happy. Not only do you deserve to be happy, but the key to your happiness is in your own hands.

You can and must learn to accept happiness and allow yourself to experience the good things in life. You must also learn to ease up on yourself when you screw up. You can begin by keeping track of your thoughts, beliefs, and feelings when you get angry. This will not be easy at first, since much of the thought process has become automatic and outside your conscious thought. But give it a try. Stop pulling your own tail!

9

KEEP THE GARBAGE OUT
let go of your distorted thinking

As I hope you're beginning to see, a good deal of maladaptive thinking and behavior comes from having a distorted view of the world. Remember what we learned about the many faces and experiences of anger in the first part of this book: Angry men see the world and the people in it differently than other people do, and this plays a key role in the way they behave and in their own unhappiness. I'd now like to move on to the next step on your way toward a better life. Let's examine exactly what these misperceptions are and look at ways to get beyond them.

Angry men have a bad habit of distorting the meaning of events around them as well as the intentions and thoughts of others. As a result, angry men live life based on faulty information. It's a lot like the explanation that computer programmers give when their programs don't work right: "Garbage in, garbage out."

In other words, you can't make good decisions if you are starting out with bad information. Your actions will not be effective and you will be prone to mistakes and poor judgment. Psychologists have names for various kinds of distorted thinking; these "distortions of logic" are listed below. See if you recognize any of these tendencies in yourself. Often it's helpful just to recognize specifically what it is that you do to skew your take on the world. At the end of this list, I'll give you an exercise that shows you how to use your newfound knowledge to break down your actions and reactions, just like we did in the last chapter.

Mind-reading

A common misperception that many angry men have is that "I know what you're thinking." This is ridiculous. No one can ever know what another person is thinking. You may have an opinion about someone else's thoughts, and you may be accurate much of the time. But you can never know for certain what another person is thinking.

Mind-reading is the belief that you *know* what another person is thinking.

"You're not really sorry. You're just saying that to shut me up."

"I didn't ask him if he was mad at me. I could just tell."

Mind-reading is maladaptive for several reasons. If you assume that you know what someone else is thinking, you are going to be wrong most of the time. And any decision that you make, anything that you try to accomplish, is likely to go wrong because you put garbage information into the decision-making machine—your brain.

Even worse, your tendency to mind-read will be exacerbated by your tendency to assume the worst. As we know, angry men often believe that others do not approve of them or think highly of them. So, more than likely, when you assume that you know what another is thinking, you will assume that the person is thinking negative thoughts about you. More garbage in. When you react to those around you on the basis of what you believe they are thinking, rather than their true thoughts, you will be hurt and angry for very little good reason. Garbage out.

Mind-reading is also frustrating to those around you. Friends, coworkers, and family can see that you are getting angry with them, but they have no idea why. The intensity of your anger isn't justified by anything that they have said or anything that has recently happened. They are genuinely mystified. This causes them to become nervous, frustrated, and possibly angry with *you*, all of which leads to more anger on your part. Pretty soon, they will be afraid to say anything to you for fear of setting you off. They will feel uncomfortable and inhibited whenever they are around you. You will begin to notice that your wife seems to laugh and have fun with others but not with you, and this will cause you to become even more angry.

Another aspect of mind-reading is expecting other people to read your mind.

"I shouldn't have to tell her I love her, she should just know."

This is a particularly common complaint from angry men when it comes to talking about their emotions. Angry men don't like to talk about their emotions, yet they want others to respect their emotions. In other words, angry men expect others to know what they are feeling and be sympathetic, but they don't want to discuss these feelings. Then, when their emotional needs are not met, they become hurt, frustrated, and angry.

Jeff's friends go off for a weekend golf trip every year. Jeff went with them for the first couple of years, but he quit going because he's not as good a golfer as the rest of them and he finds this embarrassing. After turning down their invitations several years running, Jeff realized that his friends had quit asking him to go with them. And then he started to mind-read. He assumed that they didn't want him to go because they didn't like him. Once he convinced himself that his friends disliked him, Jeff then began to avoid them, which led to fewer invitations of any kind from them. Now Jeff has convinced himself that all of his former friends have turned against him. He has never asked his former friends why they quit inviting him. He just assumes he knows. And he is wrong.

The obvious lesson here is to try to avoid mind-reading. If you find yourself beginning to believe that you "know what they're thinking," stop it! You *don't* know. You *can't* know. You have to start asking other people what they are thinking or what their opinions are. And here's the trick: Give them time to answer your question completely. Don't cut them off as soon as you hear one little statement that seems to confirm your negative opinion.

No matter how much you believe you know what someone else is thinking, *you don't*. No matter how much you want others to respect your feelings, *they cannot read your mind*. You must ask others what they are thinking and feeling, and you must tell others what you are thinking and feeling.

the myth of "should"

There is probably no single word in the English language that causes angry men more unhappiness than the word "should." The only function of this black/white word is to produce guilt in yourself and in others.

"I should have worked harder on that project."

"I should never make mistakes."

"People shouldn't park illegally in the handicapped spaces."

Nothing is gained by telling yourself what you or other people *should* have done. You are not accomplishing anything. You are just making yourself angry. The psychologist Albert Ellis refers to this type of thinking as "*must*urbation." In other words, habitual, unproductive, self-stimulation.

Black/White Thinking

Black/white thinking is a tendency to simplify events, statements, or people into artificial categories. For example, many of my patients will report that they "do not have any use for casual friends." They have one or two close friends with whom they feel somewhat relaxed, but they have nothing much to do with anyone else. Many angry men do not have a 1 to 10 scale of closeness when it comes to friends. Everyone is either a 1 (not a friend) or a 10 (an intense friend).

Black/white thinking invades many aspects of angry men's lives. Angry men often feel that people should do their jobs perfectly or not at all. This leads many of them to prefer to do more than their share of work because other people don't measure up to their standards. Opinions are either right or they are wrong. A statement is either the blunt, brutal truth or it is a lie.

This style of thinking is distorted. In reality, the world is not black and white; it's usually various shades of gray. Most opinions probably contain portions of truth (if we could ever know what "the truth" really is). And statements can communicate important aspects of the truth without being harsh, blatant, or hurtful.

Not surprisingly, black/white thinking damages relationships with other people. If you practice this particular type of distorted thinking, you probably find yourself frequently disappointed by other people, and you probably get your feelings hurt by those who you "thought were your friends." You probably feel betrayed if one of your friends disagrees with your opinion—in your mind, a true friend would agree with everything that you believe. And once you feel let down, you have no room for the "supposed friend" in your life. He gets removed from the category of "friend" and placed into the category of "not a friend."

By trying to adhere to the impossible black/white rule, angry men frequently finds themselves stubbornly defending their opinions to the death. To compromise, even in small matters, feels like admitting that they are wrong. They will rehash an argument, time after time, and wear out their wives or friends or coworkers over "a matter of principle." What is probably closer to the truth is that if angry men cannot get the other person to give in, they feel as though everyone thinks that they are wrong. Remember, angry men believe that if they are wrong, there must be something bad or inferior about them.

Black/white thinking is a form of rigidity. There are not very many situations in which rigidity is a plus. Rigidity causes bridges to collapse and branches to break off during a storm. Successful businessmen, politicians, engineers, and spouses are those who can adapt their strategies to shifting conditions. This is not to say that you should not be a man of principle; everyone should have a code to live by. What it does mean is that you should not rigidly oversimplify things that are complex. Try to become more adaptable in your thinking and in your behavior. You'll see that a lot of the most interesting and satisfying things in life tend to lie in the gray areas.

Overgeneralizing

Closely related to black/white thinking is the tendency to overgeneralize. This means that angry men are apt to focus on one small piece of evidence and draw their conclusions, ignoring all the rest of the information. It means that you take a specific example and draw general con- clusions (*all* supervisors are assholes, just because you have had an ex- perience with one disagreeable manager). It is another example of trying to live your life and make your decisions based upon inaccurate infor- mation—another example of garbage in, garbage out. When you over- generalize, you act as though the world is simpler than it really is. You assume that all situations are the same when they are not.

Just because you had one tough meeting, it doesn't mean the whole day was bad. One rainy day doesn't mean that your vacation was ru- ined. Just because your wife doesn't feel like making love one night, it doesn't mean that she doesn't love you. The process of overgeneraliza- tion is not limited to expectations. Angry men also tend to generalize their behavior. That is, angry men often respond to all or most situa- tions in ways that are appropriate only for some situations. For exam- ple, it is appropriate to be very assertive and somewhat competitive in many work situations, but if you act that way outside of work, you will come across as pushy and hostile. It is probably necessary to count your change if you buy something from a street vendor in Istanbul or Rome; it is probably not necessary to do so when you buy your wife a diamond at Tiffany's!

Many angry men have had the experience of growing up in an angry, argumentative households. Later, as adults, they have trouble handling it when others disagree with them. Do you become instantly defensive and suspicious whenever anyone asks you a question or doesn't instantly agree with something that you say? You may be over- generalizing from past experiences. Do you begin to check yourself for mistakes whenever you are around people you don't know well? If so, you are overgeneralizing, putting more garbage into the system. Garbage is bound to come out in the form of errors of judgment, more anger on your part, and more alienation from those around you. You will be getting angry around many people even though they have done nothing to you.

People *are* predictable to some extent. We all base our behavior on what we expect from certain people, certain situations, and certain events. However, the angry man acts as though people and situations are *perfectly* predictable. And they are not.

Selective Abstraction

Not only do angry men tend to overgeneralize from one small incident and make sweeping predictions, but they also tend to focus their attention almost entirely on the negative things in the world. This form of distortion is known as *selective abstraction*. This particular form of garbage input produces more than its share of garbage output. Focusing on the worst in life makes angry men bitter and pessimistic. If you can do nothing else to work on your anger, avoiding this distortion will go a long way.

The fact that you had a bad day at work should not overshadow the fact that you've had 25 good or neutral days prior to this. Many angry men seem to have a homing device that precisely guides their attention to anything that goes wrong, is out of place, or doesn't look perfect. In order to conquer your anger, you must learn to be more balanced in your evaluations of people, events, and yourself.

As Scott comes home from work one day, his 6-year-old daughter Rose runs out to show him the picture that she had drawn in school. Almost before she can speak, Scott says, "Rosie, you've got dirt all over your dress. Why can't you ever stay clean?"

"But Daddy, look at my picture."

"It's very nice, Rosie, but c'mon, we have to get you cleaned up."

Scott is missing an important moment with his daughter because all he can focus on is one tiny thing that's out of place.

When you watch your son play sports, do you tend to notice the things he screwed up? Can you remember every time your wife has criticized you? I'll bet you don't remember her compliments nearly as well.

Selective abstraction is a distortion that I am particularly prone to. I have been remodeling the old house that we live in for 10 years now. When I finish a project, I have to fight against my tendency to focus on all the little imperfections. All I see are the corners that don't meet perfectly and the paint that didn't go on quite smoothly enough. I don't notice that overall, the work looks pretty good and, besides, the place is a damn sight better than it was when we bought it.

It will take some effort at first. But if you are ever to get control over your anger and move toward a happier life, you must learn to be more balanced in your appraisal of the world.

Catastrophizing

Catastrophizing is the tendency to exaggerate just how bad things really are. Angry men can go on for hours about how bad things are. Minor irritants are described as major insults. Setbacks are described as disasters. If there is a dark cloud behind that silver lining, angry men will find it.

Remember that your patterns of self-talk have the power to influence the way you think. If you always focus on the worst, expect disaster, and "make mountains out of molehills," you will actually feel like nothing good ever happens in your life.

"It's *terrible* that I didn't get an A on my test."

"We haven't made love in a week. I don't think she loves me any more."

"If we don't get to the ball game in time to get a good seat, we might just as well stay home."

"I fell off of the wagon and had a drink. Now I might just as well get drunk."

None of these statements is factually true. They just *feel* true to angry men. This type of distorted thinking can be self-fulfilling. If you continually magnify the bad things that happen in life (everyone's life, not just yours), your pessimism will drive others away from you, cause you to miss out on opportunities, and make it more likely that the rest of the day *will* be "ruined."

Let's go back to Dave and Carl from earlier in the book. Dave has recently received his annual performance evaluation at the manufacturing plant. Even though Carl is hard on him, he knows what a good worker Dave is. As usual, the majority of Dave's performance is rated "excellent." However, in one area ("Relations with Coworkers"), Dave is rated "average." Carl explains that Dave's colleagues are reluctant to work with him on projects because he is perceived as stiff, aloof, and humorless. The other employees are also afraid to talk to Dave about routine office business because Dave becomes so sullen so easily. Even though he doesn't yell, his coworkers can always tell when he is mad. This has hampered Dave's productivity as well as the flexibility and productivity of the office as a whole.

But Dave does not interpret his "average" rating as "average." He is profoundly disturbed by the rating and immediately gets angry and defensive. He insists that his difficulties with his coworkers are more their fault than his. He insists on explicit examples of his difficult relations with his colleagues and attempts to convince Carl that none of the examples are valid. He leaves Carl's office angry, humiliated, and depressed.

Over the next several weeks, Dave cannot get his mind off of his performance evaluation. At first, he is primarily angry. He thinks about ways to find out who complained about him and how to get them back. He rehearses scenes in his mind in which he would confront, "tell off," and humiliate his accuser. As Dave continues to be obsessed with his review, he begins to convince himself that Carl and all of his coworkers can't stand him. This makes him feel terrible. He begins to look for "evidence" of their dislike in the way they act toward him. He is, of course, able to convince himself that there are many reasons to believe that those around him don't like him, can't stand him, maybe even hate him. This leads Dave to avoid his coworkers even more than before. Not surprisingly, his coworkers begin to see him as even more distant, unfriendly, and hostile. His distorted (catastrophized), garbage-in view of his performance evaluation sets off a chain of events that leads to more anger and further deterioration of his work relationships.

Personalization

Angry men are exquisitely sensitive and worried about others' opinions. In addition, angry men often act as though every bad thing that happens in the world is directed specifically at them. They sometimes seem to believe that God, life, and the rush hour traffic are all conspiring to make life miserable. This type of distortion is known as *personalization*.

Personalization is the tendency to interpret each experience, each conversation, each facial expression as personal critique, as a clue to your worth and value. This is a distortion because most events, actions, conversations, and remarks have nothing to do with you. Relax! Other people are not as concerned about you as you are. When your wife swoons over Robert Redford or Brad Pitt, it doesn't mean that she is not attracted to you. When people disagree with you about which candidate would make a better president, they are not indicating that you are stupid. When your friend buys an Orvis fly rod and not a Fenwick like yours, it doesn't mean anything about what he thinks about you as a person. When your car overheats, it is not out to get you.

Angry men are also personalizing when they compare themselves to others. Angry men are always evaluating their worth and accomplishments against those of others. And they rarely think that they measure up.

"I'm the worst basketball player in the gym."

"Everyone listens to what she says and no one listens to me."

"Everyone else seems to be relaxed at the party. What's wrong with me?"

Comparing yourself to others wouldn't be so bad if these appraisals were accurate. But remember, angry men are not balanced when it comes to self-appraisal. Angry men tend to magnify the bad and minimize the good. Most of the time, you will come out on the down side when you compare yourself to others. This type of garbage-in is a form of egocentricity. You can become so focused on evaluating everything in terms of how it relates to you that you lose sight of other people's opinions and viewpoints.

Try to remember that everyone has misfortune in their lives, not just you. Everyone gets flat tires and spills soup on their ties. Disagreements are not a comment on your intelligence. People who act annoyed in your presence are not necessarily annoyed at you. And if they are annoyed with you, so what? It's not the end of the world. Try not to take everything so personally.

Emotional Reasoning

One final area of distorted logic that is common in angry men is emotional reasoning. *Emotional reasoning* is the tendency to believe that what you feel must be true. If you *feel* stupid, then you must *be* stupid.

"If I feel guilty, then I must have done something wrong."

The problem with emotional reasoning is that emotions are not always directly related to events. Emotions are often the products of your thoughts. For example, if you feel ugly when you look in the mirror, it is because you think to yourself, "I'm ugly." There is no absolute standard for who is ugly and who is beautiful. Just because you feel a certain way, it doesn't mean that you *are* that way. If you feel inferior to financially successful people, it doesn't mean that they are better people than you are or even that they think that you are inferior (which is mind-reading,

no one is to blame

Angry men seem to have a need to blame someone for every unpleasantness. Either they blame themselves for every mistake they make, not to mention the things their children or spouses do, or they quickly look for someone or something else to blame for whatever goes wrong. There is a saying that is relevant here: "Shit happens." It is not always necessary to determine whose fault it is.

Blaming is where many arguments start and where many friendships and marriages end. Both parties try to avoid blows to their self-esteem by blaming the other. But what is accomplished by blaming? Maybe you feel relieved in the short-run to place the blame on someone else. But blaming someone else makes you angry with them, and blaming yourself makes you angry with you. Not only that, but others don't like to be blamed either, which makes them angry with you . . . which makes you even more angry!

Blaming doesn't fix problems or prevent future problems. If you are to have a happier life, you need to move beyond blaming and begin to focus on developing an objective problem-solving approach to the inevitable setbacks in life. Analyze the situation to determine how the same problem can be avoided in the future. If the event was out of your control (as most events are), accept it as bad luck. If it was in your control, ask yourself the more productive question, "What can I do to prevent this from happening next time?"

right?). Just because you feel as though all the red lights in the world are waiting for your car, it doesn't mean that they are.

The point is that your feelings are not directly linked to events in the world. Rather, they are tied to your *interpretations* of those events. For example, many angry men assume that whenever their wives or girlfriends are not in a happy mood, it must be because they have done something to make her angry or sad. An angry man will continually ask the poor woman "What's wrong? What did I do?" and won't believe it when she says that nothing is wrong. He has been conditioned to believe that when those around him are displeased or unhappy, he must be the cause. Because he *feels* responsible for her moods, the angry man assumes that he *is* responsible for every melancholy moment that she has.

You have to learn not to jump to illogical conclusions based on how you feel. You have to learn to be more objective when you are forming your opinions and making your decisions. You may feel as though something must be true, but this does not make it true.

Now What?

Now that we've gone through some of the things that may be distorted in your thinking (and notice that I didn't use "bad" or "screwed up"), you are probably saying, "OK, what do I do about it?"

One way to develop a more balanced appraisal of the things that happen to you is to make a small change in the way you talk (and think) about the things that happen to you. Whenever you find yourself making a negative statement, attach the word "but" to the end and finish it with something positive, or at least accurate.

"I had a rotten day at work, BUT . . . I can't wait to play with the kids tonight."

"The car battery died, BUT . . . at least I can afford a new one."

There is nothing wrong with acknowledging the trials and tribulations in your life. But you will be a downer to yourself and others if you don't give equal time to the positive. And there *are* positive things! You just aren't used to looking for them This is not the same thing as the popular notion of "positive thinking." You are not going to fool yourself by pretending that bad things are not bad. However, angry men often focus only on the negative and rarely give equal time to the pleasant side of life.

In the last chapter, you began to keep a record of your anger and the events and beliefs that are associated with your anger. Now you need to change the type of record that you are keeping.

Continue to record the times that you find yourself getting angry, but now try to determine whether your anger is due to any of the types

Changing your distorted thoughts: an exercise

Recognizing these thoughts isn't as difficult as it might seem. Try this. For two weeks, keep a list of every time you get angry. In this list, include the event that made you angry, your beliefs about the other person's opinion of you in that situation, relevant aspects of the situation (for example, at work, in the grocery store, etc.), and the beliefs about yourself that the event triggered. Begin keeping this record immediately and do it faithfully. In order to keep a good record, it will be necessary to carry a small notebook with you at all times. Make your notes as soon as possible. The longer you delay, the more your "data" will be distorted by fading memory, your tendency to overanalyze the situation, your tendency to deny your emotions, or by subsequent events in your day. Here are some examples:

Example 1
Event: 7:30 a.m., got cut off in traffic on way to work. Got furious, flipped the other driver the bird, tried to catch up and cut him off.
Belief about other driver's opinion: He doesn't respect me. He doesn't care if he hurts me.
Beliefs about me: Everyone takes advantage of me. No one respects me. I'm a loser.

Example 2
Event: 6:30 p.m., arrived home from work. Wife asked how day went. Got angry.
Belief about wife's opinion: She doesn't respect me. She doesn't listen to me. She doesn't care about me. She doesn't love me.
Beliefs about me: I'm not important to her. I might as well be out of her life. She would be happier if she were married to someone else. There is something wrong with me.

of distorted thinking listed above. In addition, try to reinterpret the event and give it a more rational explanation. Continue to keep a *written* record of your anger, distortions, and reinterpretations until it becomes automatic.

This is the key to managing your anger: *Recognize* your emotions, especially your anger. *Analyze* the thoughts that are associated with your emotions. *Identify* any distortions in your thinking. And *reinterpret* your distorted patterns of thought.

If you want to reduce the amount of behavioral and emotional garbage coming out, you will have to learn how to stop putting so much distorted garbage in! Here's an example of this new exercise.

As you go through this learning process, do not assume that you will never get angry. Remember that some anger is rational and understandable. Anger is a legitimate emotion with legitimate causes and consequences. However, by combating your distorted thinking, you will be able to avoid much of your irrational and unwarranted anger.

Along with preventing unnecessary and maladaptive anger, angry men need methods to diffuse anger when it does arise and prevent themselves from acting in destructive ways. They need methods to put the genie back in the bottle once it has escaped. Read on—in the next chapter, I'll discuss methods for controlling yourself once you have become angry.

10

WATCH FOR THE STORM
stop your anger before it starts

Once you have decided to deal with your anger and once you have learned to avoid physical aggression (see Chapter 13, "Physical Violence and Anger," for tips), you will be ready to develop some more sophisticated strategies for dealing both with your anger and the events and feelings that lead to that anger. Before moving on to some of these strategies, however, one common myth needs to be discussed: "getting it out of your system."

In recent years, many people have somehow gotten the idea that it is psychologically healthy to get what's bothering you "out of your system" or "off your chest." This is usually interpreted to mean that people should express their feelings directly and bluntly. Angry men love to latch onto this as a way to justify their verbal tirades. While it is true that many angry men need to be more willing to express their feelings, angry diatribes are usually not an effective way to manage anger. People who rant and rave every time they get angry don't seem to get any better at controlling their tempers. Each time they are frustrated, disagreed with, reprimanded, or otherwise interfered with, they get hot all over again. Although people need to express some of their feelings some of the time, hostile attacks on other people are not healthy or productive ways to deal with angry feelings. What is more productive is to express and deal with the feelings that are making you mad.

Let's check in with Carl again. Instead of exploding in a tirade about the broken machine, Carl could have said, "Dave, I asked you to have that machine fixed by today. What seems to be the holdup? I've got a big order to fill by next week, and I'm getting concerned that we're not going to make our ship date." In this example, Carl is letting Dave know that he is worried. For Carl, as for many angry men, being worried about something frequently leads to anger. If he had taken this approach, Dave could have told him that he had diagnosed the problem with the machine, ordered the necessary parts, and was expecting them in by that morning, in plenty of time to have the machine fixed. Carl would have had his worries eased. Dave would not have been embarrassed in front of his subordinates. And the entire working atmosphere in the plant would have been more pleasant.

The point is that Carl has no problem expressing his anger. His trouble is expressing the feelings that come before and lead to his anger. These are the feelings that need to be talked about, and these are precisely the feelings that most men, especially angry men, have trouble talking about.

Now let's take a look at Dave's reaction to being yelled at. He says nothing . . . verbally. But anyone can look at him and know exactly how angry he is. His teeth are clenched (and maybe his fists as well), his eyes stare ahead coldly, and his whole body is rigid and tense. His anger doesn't come exploding out of him. Instead, it percolates inside like a 55-gallon drum of toxic waste. In addition to his immediate reaction, he has frequent trouble with a sore back and stiff neck, even though he is only 35 years old and in great physical shape. He is often moody and distant from his wife and friends. People say that it's just a matter of time before Dave explodes or has a heart attack, because he doesn't yell and scream when he's angry.

But let's suppose that he yelled right back at Carl, "You ignorant son-of-a-bitch. I can't fix your machine until the parts get here." Not only will he not feel any better, but he'll probably lose his job. Again, it's not the anger that needs to be expressed here, but the feelings that lead to Dave's anger. For example, he could invite Carl out to lunch and tell him, "Look Carl, I know you're worried about the production schedule. But I can't work miracles. I know exactly what's wrong with the machine and I've ordered the parts. They've been sent by overnight shipping and are due in any time. We should have no trouble getting the machine fixed by the end of the day."

That may defuse some of Carl's hostility in the short run. But obviously, it doesn't deal with the way Carl treats Dave, nor does it have much effect on Dave's anger. Dave must also learn to deal with the feelings and situations that produce his anger. It is up to Dave to tell Carl how he feels when Carl humiliates him. "Carl, I'm tired of you yelling at me every time something goes wrong, especially in front of the men. From now on, please speak to me respectfully, and I will do the same for you." This may have absolutely no effect on the way Carl behaves. But it will certainly have a better chance of producing change than saying nothing.

Again, the feelings that lead to anger need to be expressed. You must learn to identify your frustration, humiliation, and worry; acknowledge these feelings to yourself and others; and deal with the circumstances producing these emotions before you get angry. For most angry men, "expressing their anger" only produces more anger.

Provocative Situations

The big step in controlling your angry responses is to anticipate anger-provoking situations and make plans to deal with them before they happen. While not every anger-producing situation can be predicted, many can. Certain people tend to make men angry. Certain situations are almost guaranteed to make them angry. And certain emotions reliably lead to the secondary reaction of anger. With a little thought and practice, many of these scenarios can be anticipated and defused before they lead to explosions.

Remember Eddie, the Debater? He works with a woman, Pauline, who he finds extremely irritating. She always seems to make jokes at Eddie's expense, brings attention to his mistakes at work, and is just plain obnoxious. Eddie hates to be in meetings with her and is uncomfortable in her presence. He finds that when he is around Pauline, he is continually justifying himself and his actions, even when no one is asking for justification. Pauline also makes Eddie extremely self-conscious. Whenever she is around, he immediately starts to worry about making mistakes, showing emotion, or revealing any vulnerabilities. This constant wariness is exhausting and makes Eddie grouchy, so that he is more likely to slip up. Also, by continually watching himself, he is constantly focusing on his shortcomings, thus magnifying them in his mind. To Eddie, Pauline is a

Provocation exercise: list your irritants

Eddie must focus on changing his own behavior and the situations that produce his anger. He starts by acknowledging that any time he is in Pauline's presence, he is likely to be irritated. Like Eddie, you should sit down, take some time, and make a list (preferably written) of the people and circumstances that reliably provoke your anger. Eddie's list includes Pauline, his brother-in-law Chuck, shopping, being judged or evaluated, paying bills, and playing golf. After you have come up with your list, acknowledge to yourself that your old ways of handling these situations have not worked and that you have got to do something different. Don't get hung up on whether or not you should have to change; just realize that you can't change other people. So, if you want to be happier, you will have to change yourself and the situations that make you angry.

After you have made your list, pick out the specific characteristics of these people and situations that provoke anger in you. Eddie knows that Pauline makes him angry, but he has never

stimulus for instant nervousness, irritability, self-criticism, and self-doubt. Eddie is self-critical by nature anyway (after all, he is an angry man!) and doesn't need another excuse to concentrate on his shortcomings.

So what can Eddie do? His temptation as a Debater is to find the ultimate wisecrack or insult that will "put that bitch in her place." However, after years of verbal bantering, Pauline still irritates him. Obviously, trying to silence Pauline by out-debating her is not a good strategy—it focuses on trying to change or control someone else's behavior, an impossible task. You cannot control others. When you try, all you get is frustrated.

When he finds that he cannot control Pauline, the only other thing that Eddie can think to do is to avoid her. Avoidance is an effective strategy in a few, limited circumstances (such as when you fear that you will physically assault someone). However, avoiding Pauline means that

stopped to think about why. When he looks into his reaction to Pauline more intensively, he realizes that she is threatening to him. She always seems to know the things that Eddie does not do well and the issues that he worries about the most. She seems to be able to sense his "hot buttons" and does not hesitate to push them. He always feels embarrassed, or defensive, or worried about what she will say next.

You will probably find that many of your anger-producing situations make you angry because they are potentially humiliating or seem to make you look bad in front of others. But there may be other things, too. Maybe you feel that you are being taken advantage of. Maybe you are getting frustrated because people or circumstances are blocking some of your goals. Your list will be different from Eddie's and from the lists of all other angry men. But it is important for you to get as specific as you can about just what it is about these people and situations that makes you so angry. Once you have determined the specific irritants, you will be ready to change the script.

Eddie must avoid anyone she is with as well as the settings where she is found. Thus, Eddie may end up avoiding other people and many important circumstances, such as meetings. And this can feed into another tendency of angry men, which is to isolate themselves from others. If you frequently try to deal with frustration by avoiding the source of frustration, you avoid more and more people and situations. So, it seems that other methods need to be considered.

Jokes and Teasing

One of the first things that you can do to make your life a bit less tense is to develop the ability to laugh at yourself, even if you have to pretend

Handling irritating people: an exercise

Many provocative situations are so repetitive that they could almost be predicted, word for word. Take advantage of this fact to plan and rehearse a different script. For example, every Monday morning, Pauline asks Eddie what he did over the weekend. Pauline, who is single and adventuresome, tends to have active and interesting weekend activities. Eddie, who is married and a homebody, enjoys relaxing on his weekends. Pauline's questioning tends to make Eddie feel boring, unimaginative, and therefore, inferior. Instead of telling Pauline, for the thousandth time, that he spent the weekend watching football on TV, Eddie could write a new script and rehearse it.

In reply to her question, "What did you do this weekend, Eddie?," Eddie could say, "The usual. You know me, Pauline. What did you do?" Pauline will probably take off on her usual litany of hang gliding, bungee jumping, and sex with strangers in an airplane bathroom. But Eddie has removed the focus from him and placed it on Pauline. If Pauline persists, so can Eddie. "Pauline, I

at first. You are a human being, which means that you will make mistakes. Some of these mistakes will be funny. In addition, people will sometimes tease you and make you the subject of jokes. If you can act as though the teasing and the normal mistakes don't bother you, two things will happen.

First, those doing the teasing will lay off sooner. Second, you will actually become more confident with yourself and other people. Your need to appear flawless will slowly diminish. You will become more comfortable with yourself because you will have found that nothing bad happens when you let yourself relax a bit. Remember, teasing is just teasing, period. Just because it sometimes makes you feel inferior doesn't mean that you *are* inferior. This will have several benefits for you. If you don't

can't believe that such an active person as you can continue to be interested in my boring weekends." Rehearsing likely conversations in advance makes it more likely that you will say the things that you want to say when you want to say them. It is difficult for most people to do this spontaneously, especially when they are angry.

Don't make the mistake of planning better "comebacks." This will just keep you in the same rut as before. The key is to rehearse a different script for the conversation. You might even want to get your wife or a friend to help you rehearse. This will provide you with the added benefit of support from another person in your attempt to change your life, in addition to more realistic practice.

You should also arrange an "escape hatch," a way for you to get out of a situation that is getting uncomfortable. It can be as simple as "Well, you'll have to excuse me. I'm way behind today and I have to get back to work." Try to arrange things so that you have a graceful way to remove yourself from a difficult situation. But again, make sure you plan your exit in advance.

get angry, the teaser will probably get tired of teasing you. If you can laugh along with a joke, you show the world (and yourself) that you are self-confident. If you can laugh at your small mistakes, they stay small. They don't become more of an issue than they need to be.

Humor is a good way to defuse anger. If something or someone is making you angry, find a way to make a joke out of it. If you spill coffee on your clean shirt, you will be much less angry and embarrassed if you can make a joke about your 10 thumbs or the abstract art on your shirt. If someone seems to be calling attention to your faults, agree with them, but to ridiculous lengths. For example, I have big feet, a fact that many of my friends used to tease me about. It used to make me mad. But now when I encounter someone who wants to tease me about them, I trot out all

Frustration exercise: say what you're feeling

One technique for dealing more effectively with frustration is to let people know when their behavior frustrates you. It is important for you to tell your boss, wife, children, and friends the effect that their treatment of you has upon your feelings. For example, you could say to your wife, "Look, Wendy, when you discuss my mistakes with our friends, it embarrasses me and makes me angry. I wish you wouldn't do that." You have to learn to express the feelings that lead to anger. This is much more important than "letting it all out" once you have become angry. Dealing with frustration is easier and safer than trying to calm back down once you have become angry. And many of the people in your life will be willing to change the way they interact with you if you let them know calmly and respectfully what effect their actions are having on you.

Frustration involves obstructions between you and your goals. Many times, these roadblocks will be surmountable and you will be able to achieve your goals. You may have to change your tactics and rethink your strategies, but you will ultimately succeed. You will reduce your frustration level if you learn to try different solutions to problems when your first attempt does not succeed. There is always

the usual, lame jokes before he has a chance to. I extol the virtues of big feet, noting that I could save money by not buying water skis, that I have less trouble retracing my footprints in the snow, that I can get a better deal per pound when I buy shoes, etc.

Humorous imagery can also be effective in defusing your anger. It is harder to stay mad at an overbearing boss if you can imagine him with a clown face complete with big, red nose.

Along with learning to laugh at yourself, you need to stop staring at your own bellybutton. There is a tendency for angry men to develop a

more than one way to skin a cat. Don't keep trying the same failed solutions to a problem over and over again.

Other obstacles are not surmountable. Sometimes you will not be able to attain your goals. When this is the case, acknowledge it and move on. This is not to say that you should give up your hopes and dreams without a good fight. But some disappointments have to be accepted with grace and dignity. You will not always succeed. Those who always succeed aren't setting their goals high enough—the only people who do not experience failure are those who do not take any risks. But don't keep trying the same old, worn-out strategies for the same old problems. If you keep banging your head against life's brick walls, all you will get is a flat head, and continual frustration and anger. Learn to pick your battles. Bold captains win more battles, but wise generals win more wars. Angry men need to learn to recognize those obstacles that can be overcome and those that cannot, and then treat them accordingly.

form of psychological egocentricism. In other words, you can get so focused on yourself, how you are treated, or how things look to you, that you lose sight of the fact that other people aren't all that concerned about you. Other people are primarily concerned about their own lives and not yours. By and large, they are not trying to "get" you, make you angry, cheat you, or otherwise harm you. Other people have their own issues and motivations that usually have nothing to do with you. Fight your tendency to see the world only through the narrow perspective of how it relates to you.

Frustration

In addition to anticipating provoking situations and changing the script, you must learn to identify the emotions that come before anger. When the world does not behave the way they want it to, despite their best efforts, angry men feel powerless. Another name for this feeling of powerlessness or helplessness is frustration.

Frustration is one of the most predictable causes of anger. When things don't go right—when you bang your elbow or get a flat tire—you get frustrated. If you don't have strategies for dealing with this frustration, it never quite goes away. This frustration simmers, waiting for any small provocation to explode into anger. For many men, the battle is lost at that point. Once they become angry, they lose their self-control and lash out in response to any minor event. Women often unknowingly walk into this dangerous situation and suffer the consequences.

Conflicts of Opinion

Angry men have a hard time with change, especially when it comes to changing their opinions. They feel a need to stick with their opinions to the bitter end because to them, changing their mind is like admitting that they were wrong. Similarly, if someone disagrees with them, angry men feel as though something must be wrong with their opinion and therefore with them.

An important factor in controlling your anger is to realize that others' disapproval of something you do or disagreement with something you think is not the same thing as disapproval of you as a person. Just because someone disagrees with your taste in ties or your political opinions doesn't mean that they think you are stupid or otherwise inferior. It doesn't mean that you are wrong or stupid. It doesn't mean that you have to defend yourself.

Telling the Truth

Many angry men have a fierce pride in their integrity. In fact, many arguments get started when an angry man thinks that someone doesn't believe something that he said. "Are you calling me a liar?"

Conflict exercise: don't try to win

Practice having discussions with people in which you don't try to "win" an argument or badger them into agreeing with you. Useful phrases for this purpose include "I can see why you would think that," "That makes sense, too," and "I guess that's why they make lots of different neckties." Focus on discussing rather than winning. If you are not always focused on winning, you won't have to be so worried about losing.

In order to have these open-minded discussions, you must give the other person time to speak. You have to discipline yourself to listen to the other person. Try not to interrupt with contradictions or comebacks. Angry men try to dominate and control conversations because they are afraid of where the conversations will go. It is important to truly listen to what the other person has to say. And the purpose of your listening should not be to find a hole or flaw in what the other person has to say. Practice being sincerely interested in what is being said. You may learn something new, make a new friend, or just enjoy a stimulating exchange of ideas. In most situations, there is no "right" answer, only different opinions.

Angry men pride themselves on being blunt with the "truth" and become insulted when they don't receive instant and complete agreement from others. "I speak my mind. If people can't handle it, that's their problem." "I tell it like I see it." However, they are usually blunt with only part of the truth. They can be quite challenging and aggressive when they feel uncomfortable, rather than honestly acknowledging their discomfort. They are quick to point out when someone else has made a mistake, but are reluctant to admit when they are wrong. They have difficulty complimenting, being tender, or acknowledging fear, all of which are aspects of the "truth." In short, angry men often have a rather narrow idea of what honesty and integrity involve. This limited perspective on the truth contributes to their anger.

There is much to enjoy and praise in the world and in other people. Until you develop the confidence to acknowledge the positive as well as the negative, you aren't truly "speaking the truth." Be as bold and up front with your praise as you have been with your criticism. Be as willing to tell someone when they have made you happy as you are when they make you angry. When you disagree with someone, you should do so in a straightforward and honest way. But being truthful does not mean that you have to be tactless, challenging, or aggressive. There is a difference between speaking the truth and being harshly blunt.

Let's go back to Eddie. During a recent meeting, Pauline gave a small presentation, followed by some recommendations for change in the department. Eddie noticed several factual errors in Pauline's data as well as some misinterpretations. When asked his opinion, Eddie replied in his usual blunt manner, of which he is proud, "You got your facts wrong and your analyses are worthless. You've wasted our time in this meeting because you did a superficial, half-ass job." Eddie is technically correct. Pauline got some data wrong and probably did not put enough effort into her presentation. But what has Eddie accomplished by his attack on Pauline? He has humiliated her, thus perpetuating their antagonistic relationship. He has probably ruined any chance of he and Pauline working together in the near future, which reduces their effectiveness and value to the company. Has he helped Pauline get the correct data or improve her analyses for the future? No. Has he contributed to the welfare of the company? No. But he has made others wary of him for fear of similar treatment. Not only that, but Pauline and the others are going to be giving Eddie a wide berth, isolating him and possibly contributing to his anger in the long run. And Pauline will be sure to take advantage of any future opportunity to make Eddie look bad.

An equally "honest" appraisal could have been delivered much more tactfully, in a manner that acknowledged both the good and bad points of Pauline's presentation. "Pauline, you've hit the cost analysis right on the head. But I've come up with some recent figures that are different from yours. Maybe we should sit down and sort through the new data and see if you need to modify your analyses." This style delivers the same message, "You've made some mistakes," without humiliating Pauline. Why is this style preferable? First, Pauline is less likely to be angry with Eddie and thus less likely to provoke him in the future. This is a good example of Eddie managing his anger-provoking situations. Second, Eddie sees himself acting in a mature, upbeat, and assertive yet respectful manner, and this is good for his self-image. Third, this more positive way of criticizing Pauline will make it more likely that Eddie's coworkers will want to work with him. It feels good to be wanted by other people, even in small matters. When you make changes in your life and they work out, you will feel good!

Profanity

Profanity instantly intensifies any discussion or argument. You can see this in televised sports all the time. Two basketball players come up from a fall and begin to argue with each other. Even when you cannot hear what they are saying, you know instantly when someone uses profanity because that's when the first push or punch happens. Profanity instantly adds fuel to anger.

You may have a habit of casually using cuss words in conversation or when you are experiencing even minor frustration or irritation. You may not see the harm in it. And for others, the casual use of profanity may in fact be harmless. However, an angry man who is trying to manage his anger can't afford to express himself in that way. Profanity is not only an expression of your anger, but can also lead you to become instantly more angry.

Profanity exercise: Stop cussing

Angry men need to use any tricks that they can think of to control their tempers. There are many creative and effective ways of saying what you have to say without the use of profanity. Later, when your temper is under better control, you may choose to join in with the rest of the locker room talk.

Put It All into Perspective

If you behave in angry ways, you will be more likely to feel angry. The idea that behavior can cause feelings is the opposite of we usually believe. Most of us believe that people act angry because they feel angry. While this is true, it is also the case that when you act angry, you will feel angrier. Yelling, pointing your finger at someone during an argument, sulking, and punching walls will make you feel angrier than you did before. Change the script.

So, it is useful to anticipate anger-provoking situations, prepare a different script (not a better insult), rehearse your new script prior to the situation, and have an escape hatch if you feel yourself losing control.

In your effort to change the situations that are contributing to your anger, you should try to analyze these situations objectively. When we were in graduate school, my wife and I seemed to be having arguments every day after work. The arguments were usually pointless and usually began over trivial issues. I often took offense at some minor disagreement of my wife's and my anger would quickly escalate. During a calm time, we sat down and tried to analyze this pattern. I had to admit that I usually came home tense and worn out from work. Similarly, my wife revealed that her job was stressful, too. Many days, people disagreed with her all day at work, forcing her to defend her opinions and decisions. The last thing that either of us wanted when we got home was a disagreement. So, we decided on a new rule. No discussions or debates until after dinner. This gave us both an hour or two to relax, change into more comfortable clothes, and get something to eat. This dramatically reduced the number and intensity of our arguments.

There are many other examples of altering the circumstances of your life so that they are less provocative. If it makes you mad when the paperboy throws your paper in the same puddle day after day, why not put up a curbside box and tip him to put the paper in it? Don't get hung up on the fact that he should do it right without a tip. Of course he should. But the fact is, a small tip is likely to get you the result you want and reduce your anger. If you get hung up in traffic on your way home from work, choose a different route. It might take a little longer, but you will be in a better mood when you get home. If you get angry with the other men in your favorite bar, find another bar. To anticipate your indignant reply, of course you have a right to go into any bar you choose. But often you have a choice between being right and being happy.

Try to see the other person's point of view. Maybe your boss is under a lot of pressure from his boss. Since he depends upon you in order to get his work done, he may be taking his own frustrations out on you. Realizing that he is not after you personally may help you to deal with him more easily. Many other times, just the realization that the other person truly believes that they are right may help you to control yourself. Again, it will allow you to see that they are not out to get you personally, they are sincerely disagreeing with your opinion, as you are with theirs. Other people don't get up in the morning and try to figure out ways to make you mad. Their obnoxious or disagreeable behavior is usually not directed at you personally. They have their own reasons for how they behave and you just happen to be in the way. Maybe they have marital problems. Maybe their hemorrhoids are especially painful today. Maybe their children are screwing up in school. Maybe you are encountering another angry man!

Remember, it is not reasonable to try to avoid all anger. Anger is an emotion. Emotions occur for reasons. However, angry men have too much, too intense, too frequent, and too violent experiences of anger. You can learn to cool it and control it.

11

BE THE SQUEAKY WHEEL
speak up to get your needs met

Angry men frequently feel as though nobody understands them, nobody cares about them, and nobody is looking out for them. You probably feel this way from time to time. Where does this feeling come from? Maybe you didn't get much adult attention, especially from men, when you were growing up. Maybe your experience of having to look out for yourself, because you had no protector, taught you that you can't trust anyone. Maybe you were neglected or, worse, abused as a child. Maybe this has caused you to shut out those who would now like to try to understand you, to care for you, to watch out for you. Maybe you feel guilty when you think about asking for help or favors from your friends and family. Maybe you think that these kinds of thoughts are "selfish."

For whatever reason, angry men often don't get their emotional needs met. They don't get the sympathy that they would like when they are down. They don't get encouragement when they would like it. They just don't feel special or cared for by other people.

Problems with Passivity

If you feel that others do not pay enough attention to your wants and desires, you need to do something about it. Remember, you cannot expect

Assertiveness exercise: don't explain, just repeat

There are certain techniques that you can learn that will make it easier for you to be assertive. The first might be called the "broken record" technique. When you are trying to be assertive with someone, very often they will insist that you explain the reasons for your demands. However, often they are not really interested in your reasons. They just want to find a way to confuse you or put you on the defensive by finding holes in your logic or leading you off on a tangent. If you have a legitimate request, you don't need to make more than a single attempt to explain your reasons. If the person continues to argue with you, do not continue to explain yourself. Just repeat your request.

For example, let's suppose that you have a neighbor with a small, obnoxious dog. And let's suppose that this dog likes to do his business in your yard, usually right under your bedroom window. In the past, you would have probably hinted to your neighbor several times that you would like him to keep his dog under better control. If your neighbor either ignored or didn't get your hints, you would get angry. But what if one day, you decided to speak plainly to your neighbor about keeping his dog out of your yard?

"Stanley, your dog has been leaving his mess in my yard and I wish you would keep him in your yard. He's a nice enough dog, but I don't like the smell of his mess." Stanley may not respond the way you want him to at first. "What are you worried about? It's good for the grass." Restrain your urge to tell Stanley off and remember to use the broken record technique. Don't explain your request, just repeat it. "Just the same, Stanley, I would like you to keep your dog out of my yard." People may not give up easily! Your neighbor may come back with, "How am I supposed to watch him 24 hours a day?" This is a ploy to try to put the responsibility of figuring out how to control his dog onto you. Don't fall for it. Stay focused on your request. Don't give in to the temptation to justify your request. Just repeat yourself! "Stanley, it's not my job to tell you how to control your dog. Please just keep him out of my yard."

By being calmly assertive, you will have succeeded in alerting your neighbor to your displeasure at the dog manure in your yard and also let your neighbor know how you would like things to change. People may not always cooperate with your requests. But there is a better chance that you will have less manure in your life than if you continue to get mad about life's annoyances but say nothing. If nothing changes when you act in an assertive manner, you will have to decide whether to take more unpleasant steps. In this case, you could decide to call the animal control department, or you may decide to just let the issue go.

Rich's company needed a new office manager and interviewed several candidates. Rich and his partner then had a meeting to decide who to hire. Rich suggested that they hire one of the applicants who had had a great deal of experience. His partner objected to the salary that she was asking and suggested that they hire a student at minimum wage. "In the long run, I think that hiring someone with experience will be cost-effective," responded Rich. "We won't have spend as much time training her, and we know from her references that she is able to run an office." "What is she going to do that a student couldn't do?" asked his partner. Again, Rich outlined his opinions about the long-term benefits of hiring an experienced office manager. And again, his partner insisted that they not spend the money for the more qualified person. At this point, Rich realized that his partner was not particularly interested in his reasons for wanting the more experienced applicant. He was set on his opinion and was not going to be swayed by any of Rich's arguments. "I think that we should hire an experienced person." "But, why?" asked his partner. "I've already given you my reasons. I think that we should hire an experienced person."

Rather than letting himself get worn down by trying to answer all of his partner's questions, Rich refused to repeatedly explain and justify himself. He may not get his way all of the time, but Rich will save himself a lot of grief in the long run and will be more likely to make positive changes in his life than if he lets himself get sidetracked into repeatedly justifying his reasonable requests.

Now don't interpret this to mean that you should never give your reasons for your opinions. But you must develop the wisdom to know when people are really interested in your reasoning and when they just want to shoot holes in anything you say. Use of the broken record technique is not meant to shut down all discussion and debate. Issues need to be discussed, and all interactions between people need a healthy give and take of ideas and opinions. But discussions often are *not* productive. Many times, the discussion is merely a cover for someone trying to impose his will on someone else, in this case, you. Many times, you will feel as though you have been cheated or otherwise manipulated by someone whose verbal skills are better than yours and by your own tendency to justify your wants and needs. Try to recognize these domineering types of discussions early on and then refuse to fall into the trap of excessive explanation. Don't explain. Just repeat.

others to read your mind. You have to let your friends and family know what you want and need. Think about the saying that "the squeaky wheel gets the grease." This means that if someone doesn't speak up, they don't get attended to. No one will know what you need unless you tell them.

Becoming more "assertive" means learning to get your needs met more satisfactorily, without aggression. It means being able to say what you want without having to get angry first. It means taking care of yourself without abusing others. People who lack assertiveness feel as though they get taken advantage of: People cut in front of them in line, others get the best assignments at work, they don't get the service that they pay for from the mechanic, and so forth.

When people fail to take action to make sure that they get taken care of fairly, we say that their behavior is passive. Passive people don't stand up for themselves. They don't take the necessary and appropriate actions that will make it more likely that they get treated with respect and consideration. Angry men are often so unsure of themselves that they don't speak up until their anger builds to the point of explosion. Then, they charge past assertiveness into an angry confrontation. They raise their voices, intimidate, and threaten. These types of behavior are called aggressive. Aggressive people take care of their own needs (at least they think that they do), but they trample on other people's rights and feelings in the process.

The reason for becoming more assertive is not just to keep people from taking advantage of you in everyday, practical matters. You also need to be assertive about your emotional needs. This means telling your wife, or your boss, or your children what you think, feel, and need in a calm, clear, and concise manner. If you would like a little more attention from your wife, you have to let her know. But do so before you get angry. If you are worried about your boss's perception of the quality of your work, ask her for regular and precise performance appraisals. If you frequently feel like no one is taking care of you the way you take care of others, maybe you need to let them know when you are hurt, anxious, or afraid. You also need to let people know when you are feeling frustrated and deal with that emotion before it leads to more anger.

It is easier and more effective to increase your assertiveness a little at a time. Start off by taking care of small issues. For example, if you get short-changed at a fast food restaurant, return to the counter and calmly insist on receiving the correct change. Don't be hostile or aggressive and do not be deterred by what you think the other customers will think of you. If you disagree with something that someone has just said, say so in a calm, constructive manner. (But be ready to change your opinion if the evidence suggests that the other person is right.) If someone cuts in front of you in line, remind him that others have been waiting longer than he has and show him where the end of the line is. But don't blow things out of proportion. If the jerk refuses to go to the end of the line, write him off for a jerk and forget it. Don't sweat the small stuff. One of the differences between assertiveness and aggressiveness is deciding which battles are worth fighting and which are not.

As you get more comfortable with letting people know what you want, you can move on to more important issues. This will involve letting the world learn more and more about you. Be more revealing about how you feel and what you would like people to do for you. If you want your wife to be proud of your promotion, let her know that her pride in you makes you proud of yourself. If you want your son to admire you, let him know that his opinion of you is important to you. If you happen to be depressed, don't isolate yourself from everyone. Let them try to sympathize with you.

This doesn't mean that you should tell everyone about *every* thought and feeling that you have. Use your judgment and common sense about who gets told what. But you must make more of yourself known to other people than you have been comfortable doing in the past. Make no mistake, however. People are not going to immediately start being more attentive to you. They have their own lives and their own needs to worry about. They are not going to be interested in hearing about your needs all the time. Use your judgment, but do let yourself be heard.

Pressure to Please

Many people are reluctant to be more assertive because they are afraid that people won't like them if they assert themselves. They are afraid that people will think of them as pushy, overbearing, or obnoxious. But if you to try to live your life to please everybody, you will continue to be frustrated. This is because what others want may not be what is good for you. Also, two different people may want you to do two different things. And then what do you do?

An example of the first dilemma is the neighbor who always borrows your tools and takes his time returning them. If you try to please him by loaning him your tools, you won't have the tools when you need them. An example of the second dilemma is when both your own family and your wife's family expect you to spend the holidays with them. You obviously cannot please both groups of people.

Asserting yourself will not upset people as much as you think it will.

Mistreatment exercise 1:
make the consequences clear

Let's look at Rich and his newfound assertiveness. He decided to try it out with his teenage son, Junior. They had had a running battle ever since Junior got his driver's license about the fact that Junior never buys gas when he borrows his father's car. Rich decided that, instead of using his usual method of chewing Junior out whenever he left the car with no gas, he would set conditions for using his car and then stick by them.

He told Junior that, in the future, if he brought the car home with less gas in it than it had when he left, Junior would 1) not be allowed to use the car for a week and 2) must fill the car up before he could use it again. Junior suffered the consequences one time and then never repeated the offense. More important, Rich did not have to get mad about the issue again. He decided how he wanted to be treated and what the consequences would be if he was not treated the way he wanted to be. He then told Junior clearly and concisely what the new rules were and calmly but firmly enforced the consequences when it was necessary.

This will not always work. Many times you have no power to enforce consequences. And many times, people continue to treat you badly, even when you have been assertive with them. For example, Junior could have continued to bring the car home empty, and suffered the consequences, week after week. If your first attempts to get treated right don't work, you may have to up the ante. You might want to tell Junior that it would now cost him two weeks of walking if he didn't put gas in the car. However, in many circumstances, you may just have to suck it up and put up with the unpleasant situation. But taking calm and assertive steps to get your needs met is preferable to repeated angry confrontations and is often more effective.

And if it does, they'll get over it. When you decide to make some changes in the way you deal with people, you will be surprised at how quickly they will get used to your new approach to life. As soon as they have had a few weeks to get used to the new you, they won't even remember what you were like before.

What people don't like and don't tolerate for very long are aggressive people. You are not allowed to take advantage of other people in order to take care of yourself. Your right to stick out your fist ends where your neighbor's nose begins. The right to stand up for yourself and look after your interests is not a blank check to pursue your own gain by any means possible. You should not, for example, confuse stating your opinion

Mistreatment exercise 2: rehearse beforehand

Just wanting to change the way you deal with people is not enough to make it happen. You have developed some pretty strong habits. You have been automatically responding with anger for a long time now. You have to use every trick that you can think of to close the barn door before the angry horse gets out.

As with the other behavior changes that you have made so far, practicing more assertive behavior in advance of situations makes it more likely that you will remember what to say when the time comes to say it. If you will be going into a meeting in which you want to make a particular point, write down what you want to say and how you want to say it. Be concise and to the point. Imagine the arguments that will be raised against your opinion and your assertive (but not aggressive) responses to those arguments. The more practice you have, even in your head, the better and more comfortable you will be when the time comes.

Imagine yourself as you would like yourself to be. More poised. More confident. Able to handle differences of opinion with-

clearly with belittling others' opinions. You should not assume that others' needs and rights are less important to them than yours are to you.

People will not always meet your needs just because you state them assertively. Just because you want something doesn't mean that other people feel the need to give it to you. When this happens, you have to decide what you will do if your needs are not met, and then you must follow through. This does not mean that you should take revenge or punish people who do not do what you want them to do. Rather, if you perceive that you are not being treated the way that you think you should be treated, then you must decide what you will do to deal with the situation.

out getting angry. Imagine yourself speaking clearly and effectively and also listening intently and respectfully. Do not be sidetracked by others' tears, hostility, accusations, or other maneuvers designed to thwart you in your attempt to stand up for yourself. Keep focused on the issues and your reasons for your demands. And above all, do not get hostile.

You should practice not only in your mind but in your behavior. Insist on the correct change if someone makes a mistake, even if it's only a penny. For now, you can use the practice. Send your steak back if it's not cooked exactly the way you like it. You can be tolerant later. For now, you need the practice. If the supermarket cashier bounces your fruit when she weighs it, explain to her that you would like her to be more gentle and then ask her to send someone back to the produce section for a replacement. Later on, you will have better judgment about when to make a stand and when to be tolerant. But for now, practice your right to assert yourself. But do so respectfully and calmly.

Self-worth and pleasure exercise: increase the positives

It is one thing to agree that you deserve to be happy and enjoy yourself. It is quite another to take active measures to see that it actually happens. Many angry men often have no regular avenues for enjoyment. They don't participate in sports. They have no hobbies. They don't travel. Lots of guys don't even use all of their vacation time. Angry men often cannot allow themselves to relax, to goof off, or play. It's no wonder that they are so unhappy.

You need to actively seek out the things that make you happy and then pursue them. If your marriage or other relationship is not giving you the satisfaction that it used to, get busy and do your part to revitalize it. This may mean marriage counseling, showing your wife more appreciation or attention, or simply spending more time with her. If you have always wanted to do some traveling, what are you waiting for? The important thing to remember is that you shouldn't wait for things to improve. You should take an active hand in shaping your own future happiness.

Don't settle for mediocrity in your marriage, in your job, or in other areas of your life. You will not always be successful. Sometimes things won't improve, despite intense effort on your part. But

Lack of Self-Worth and Pleasure

Angry men are their own worst enemies when it comes to getting their needs met. They tend to have some core beliefs that get in the way of greater assertiveness, greater happiness, and reduced anger. These beliefs about yourself and other people are different for each individual, but they tend to revolve around some common themes.

One of those themes is low levels of self-confidence. As we have

it's safe to say that more things will improve more of the time if you take it upon yourself to try to actively improve them. It is up to you and you alone to make yourself happy.

Taking control of your life starts by taking more control over yourself. If you have turned into a couch potato, get some exercise and get back into shape. Regular exercise is good for depression, anxiety, and anger. It gives a person a feeling of self-control and self-worth. When people are physically healthy, it has beneficial effects on their psychological health as well.

Other areas of your life that once may have given you pleasure or contentment need to be cultivated as well. If your church was a source of fulfillment for you, get back to it. If you used to enjoy a well-kept lawn, fire up the mower. Have you been enjoying time with your children lately? They will only be with you for a short while before they are on their own. Then it will be too late to do the things that fathers and children like to do when the kids are young (that maybe your father didn't do with you). If you do not make an effort to enjoy your children now, you will have missed opportunities for present fulfillment and future memories. Do you like to fish, do volunteer work, be active in politics? All of these are things to be pursued for the joy and fulfillment that they bring. But no one will do it for you.

noted earlier, angry men frequently feel the need to apologize or otherwise atone for themselves. This may not be a conscious process, but it can be seen in the tendency of angry men to give others "the shirt off of their back" while ignoring their own needs and happiness. It may be a bit extreme to put it this way, but do you try to buy other's approval? Is much of your behavior designed to get others to prop you up and make you feel secure or worthwhile? If so, you need to find internal ways to get those good feelings so that you rely less upon other people. Because when other people fail to provide that kind of validation for you, it can lead you to feel worthless and then angry.

Another theme that angry men seem to believe is that they should always be productive, that they should never ease up and enjoy life. They seem to think that enjoying an accomplishment is being cocky, that buying things for themselves is selfish, and that relaxing is lazy. But you have a right to enjoy life and accept pleasure. This may seem simple and self-evident, but when we start to get specific about it, you may find yourself questioning whether or not you deserve to be happy. For example, you have a right to put yourself first sometimes. Not all the time, but sometimes. You don't need to get angry or belligerent in order to do this. Remember earlier in the book when you were encouraged to be fair to yourself? This means that if you are allowed to put other people first, you are allowed to do the same for yourself at times. You get to choose the restaurant sometimes. You get to buy yourself something nice sometimes. You get to take a day off. You are allowed to relax. These are all things that many angry men have difficulty doing because they have a core belief that they are not deserving. Allowing yourself some pleasure is not selfish. This doesn't mean that you should put yourself first all of the time or spend your days totally engrossed in the pursuit of pleasure. But you can do the things that you want to do some of the time.

Another core belief that leads to low levels of confidence for many angry men is "If someone disagrees with me, I must be the one who is wrong." Just because people disagree with you doesn't mean that you are crazy or wrong. People are allowed to have their opinions and you are allowed to have yours. No one knows what the "truth" is. There are very few "facts." Get out of the habit of immediately doubting yourself as soon as someone questions you or disagrees with you. Resist the temptation to go on the offensive in order to ram your point of view down other people's throats.

A related theme is the belief that if someone disapproves of something that you have done, you must have done something wrong. It is not your job to please all of the people all of the time. Not only is this impossible, but it is frustrating as well, because you never quite know what the rules are. Trying to shape your behavior to fit others' expectations is like to trying to brush your teeth in an airplane bathroom. You never know when the floor is going to jerk underneath you, making you smear toothpaste all over your face. In addition, what is pleasing to one person (such as your boss) may not please your coworker. So you will inevitably get caught in conflicts where it seems that no matter what you do, someone gets mad at you. People are allowed to disagree with what you do; it does not mean that you are wrong. But don't automatically dismiss people's opinions, either. You will be wrong sometimes. Listen to what others have to say. But don't automatically assume that they are right and you are wrong.

PART

THREE

get real, get help

12

YOUR ANGER STATUS REPORT
sometimes self-help is not enough

What do you do if you have acknowledged your anger, taken on the responsibility for change, and faithfully tried the exercises in Part Two, but your temper is still out of control? The first thing that I would recommend is patience. You are trying to make some major changes in your life, and they will not happen overnight or all at once. You will slip up from time to time, have good days and bad days. But over the course of a month or six weeks, you should be able to look back and see some progress. You should be able to objectively see that your angry behavior occurs less often and less intensely than before. If this is not the case, if you have seen no progress, or if you think your progress has been too slow, it may be time for you to get some professional help with your anger. This section will help you determine whether your anger-related problems with physical aggression, sex, substance abuse, or depression are serious enough to require professional help. The next few chapters discuss these rather serious problems that plague many angry men. Very often, these problems are more than anyone, especially angry men, are able to handle on their own. Read these chapters with an open mind. They will include some last-ditch things that you can try to prevent disasters, like how to keep yourself from abusing others. But if after reading them, you decide that you need to get some help, do it. If you are not sure, ask your wife, your best friend, or someone else that you trust, and then take their advice!

Five Ways to Find the Right Therapist for You

1. Word of mouth. This is always one of the most reliable ways to find any kind of service, including mental health services. If you have a friend or family member that you trust, and he has good things to say about his therapist, chances are good that you will be satisfied as well.

2. Referral services. Many states have referral services that can provide you with a list of qualified psychologists in your area.

3. Recommendations from your physician. Family doctors have to deal with all types of patient problems. They usually have an opinion about who are the good specialists in the area, including psychologists.

4. Your local mental health center. Most counties have a public mental health center. The center may be able to help you with its own staff. If they cannot, they usually know reputable private psychologists.

5. Psychiatrists. Psychiatrists (mental health doctors who can dispense medication) work very closely with psychologists. They are in a good position to advise you on choosing one who will be right for you. You don't necessarily need to be going to a psychiatrist to call one up for a recommendation.

There are several forms of help that an angry man can take advantage of. First, there are counselors. Although the definition of counselor differs from state to state, there are some general characteristics of counselors across states. They will usually have a master's degree in either psychology or social work. A counselor is trained to listen to the problems that you are having, point out areas where you could make some changes, and sometimes provide exercises or advice designed to help you make these changes. A second source of professional help would be a psychologist. A psychologist is a mental health professional who has a doctorate (Ph.D.) in psychology. While a psychologist may also function as a counselor, a psychologist will usually go beyond the provision of advice and exercises and will be able to design a targeted therapeutic program to help you make the changes you desire. This program may involve counseling (advice giving), practicing behavior change, exposure to anxiety-provoking situations, and many other techniques that have been shown to contribute to the types of changes that you and many others wish to make in their behavior.

Other areas of professional assistance would include specialized drug or alcohol counselors. The level of education among these counselors can vary widely, from a high school education to a doctorate. But these counselors will have specialized training in the treatment of alcohol and drug addiction.

In addition to individual treatment, many groups, workshops, and seminars are available. These may be sponsored by a counselor or psychologist, employers, hospitals, universities, the military, churches, and many other organizations. In addition, there are specialized services such as Alcoholics Anonymous and Narcotics Anonymous. These do not necessarily involve professionals. Rather, groups such as AA rely on a set of steps for you to complete (that is why they are referred to as "12-step programs"), as well as suggestions and encouragement from other people in the group who have gone through the same problems with drugs or alcohol. While seminars and lectures can be helpful, you should not expect your problems to be solved in a workshop or lecture. You are probably going to need more help than this. These are serious issues that you are dealing with, and they require serious attention.

You will find a list of resources and referral services for specific problems at the end of this chapter.

What to Expect in Therapy

As with most people considering professional help for the first time, you may be wondering what good it will do to talk to a psychologist about your problems. The simple fact of talking to an understanding and objective person about your problems feels good to many angry men. A psychologist will keep everything you say completely confidential. In addition, he (or she) has dealt with many other people with your type of problem and may have some good suggestions of things for you to try; things that you may not have considered. Psychological therapy or counseling is a good way to experiment with new ways of thinking and behaving in a relatively safe situation before trying them out in the real world.

"What can he tell me about myself that I don't already know?" "What good does talking do?" "I don't like to talk to anyone about this kind of stuff, especially a stranger." Don't let yourself fall into these old traps. These are nothing more than excuses. The truth is that revealing your insecurities and vulnerabilities to another person makes you extremely uncomfortable, and you don't want to do it. Almost everyone is initially nervous about therapy. You will most likely be nervous, too. But be patient and persistent. The nervousness usually goes away in a few sessions. If you are still uncomfortable after a month or so, let your therapist know. It may be that you need to change what you are doing in therapy or, alternatively, that your therapist needs to change what he is doing.

There are many different approaches to therapy, but all share some common elements. Your therapist will want to see you on more than one occasion. The most common schedule is once a week for about an hour. You should not expect to get much in the way of suggestions from your therapist for the first few sessions. He will need to get to know you before he decides where to begin. And you will have to be patient. You have had years to get where you are and you can't expect radical changes overnight. Expect to spend several months at the least in therapy. Anger management is one of the most difficult areas of behavior to improve. So give it a chance. Your therapist will initially ask you many questions about yourself, your family, friends, coworkers, etc. These questions will be personal. It is important for your therapist to know all about you in order to help you, so do your best to be open and honest. Rather than hide something painful or mislead your therapist, simply tell him if you are not ready to answer any of his questions.

As therapy progresses and you become more comfortable with your therapist, you will find yourself doing more and more of the talking. Your therapist may also give you "homework" to do between sessions. This will involve exercises designed to help you change some of your old, maladaptive thinking and behavioral habits. For example, you may be asked to read a book on anger management (!). You may also be asked to experiment with new ways of talking, such as limiting yourself to "thank you" when you receive a compliment, instead of blowing it off, "explaining" yourself, or otherwise avoiding the compliment. Get in with both feet and try your best to do what your therapist asks you to do. You will make faster progress that way.

Don't be afraid to confide your emotions and thoughts with your therapist. Remember that he is not there to judge you. Unlike others with whom you have come into contact, he will not use your personal information to tease or embarrass you. His job is to help you feel better.

You are not superhuman. If you need help, don't let a distorted sense of pride stand in your way. Get the help you need. Pride is a wonderful thing, in its place. And sometimes, that place is in your pocket.

Self-Help and Mental Health Resources

Alcoholics Anonymous
www.aa.org

American Association for Marriage and Family Therapy
www.aamft.org

American Association of Suicidiology
www.suicidiology.org

American Mental Health Alliance
http://mental-health-coop.com
AMHA@mental-health-coop.com

American Psychiatric Association
1400 K Street NW
Washington, D.C. 20005
202/682-6000
202/682-6850 (fax)
www.psych.org
apa@psych.org

American Psychological Association
APA Public Affairs
750 First Street NE
Washington, D.C. 20002-4242
800/374-3120
www.apa.org

Brain Injury Association
105 N. Alfred Street
Alexandria, VA 22314
703/236-6000
www.biausa.org

Cocaine Anonymous
CAWSO, Inc.
P.O. Box 200
Los Angeles, CA 90049-8000
310/559-5833
310/559-2554 (fax)
www.ca.org
cawso@ca.org

Narcotics Anonymous
800/899-0040
www.na.org

National Alliance for the Mentally Ill
200 N. Glebe Road, Suite 1015
Arlington, VA 22203-3754
800/950-NAMI (6264)
www.nami.org

National Depressive & Manic-Depressive Association
730 N. Franklin Street, Suite 50
Chicago, IL 60610-3526
800/826-3632
www.ndmda.org

National Domestic Violence Hotline
P.O. Box 161810
Austin, TX 78731
800/799-SAFE (7233)
800/787-3224 (TDD)
www.usdoj.gov/vawo/newhotline.htm

National Institute of Mental Health
Information Resources and
Inquiries Branch
National Institute of Mental Health
Room 7C-02, MSC 8030
Bethesda, MD 20892-8030
800/421-4211
www.nimh.nih.gov

**National Mental Health
Association**
NMHA Information Center
1021 Prince Street
Alexandria, VA 22314-2971
800/969-6642
www.nmha.org

**National Organization for
Seasonal Affective Disorder**
P.O. Box 40190
Washington, D.C. 20016
www.nosad.org

**National Self-Help
Clearinghouse**
25 West 43rd Street, Suite 620
New York, NY 10036-7406
212/354-8525
www.selfhelpweb.org

Psychological Self-Help (book)
http://mentalhelp.net/psyhelp

**SA\VE (Suicide Awareness/
Voices of Education)**
P.O. Box 24507
Minneapolis, MN 55424-0507
612/946-7998
www.save.org
save@winternet.com

Sex Addicts Anonymous
ISO of SSA
P.O. Box 70949
Houston, TX 77270
800/477-8191 (10 a.m.–2 p.m. CST
Mon, Tues, Wed, Fri; 2 p.m.–6 p.m. Thu)
www.sexaa.org
info@saa-recovery.org
also provides information in Spanish

12-Step Meetings
http://12stepmeetings.com
Includes:
Alcoholics Anonymous
AlAnon
Co-Dependents Anonymous
Debtors Anonymous
Emotional Health Anonymous
Marijuana Anonymous
Narcotics Anonymous
Overeaters Anonymous
Sexaholics Anonymous
Workaholics Anonymous

13

HITTING A BRICK WALL
violence and anger: a deadly combination

I
f you're an angry man who lashes out in violence, my advice is simple: Of all the things that you have to do, you must stop the physical aggression. *You must stop hitting your wife, your children, and those with whom you disagree.* You must also stop destroying your own property and stuff that belongs to others. Punching walls, slamming doors, wild driving, and breaking things must stop. "I was mad" doesn't cut it as an excuse anymore. When that kind of energy is being released, people get hurt. Guilt, remorse, and humbly asking for forgiveness after a violent episode are no longer acceptable. "I'm sorry" doesn't fix or justify or atone for anything that you have injured or broken. You and you alone are responsible for your abuse and for stopping it. Nothing another person says is grounds for a physical assault. There are no excuses. You must learn to prevent the violence before it happens.

When you aggress against other people or their property, you are not only guilty of a moral and ethical breach, but you have probably also broken the law. According to FBI statistics, there were over 420,000 arrests of men for violent crime in 1997 (the latest year for which complete data were available). That included over 11,000 arrests for murder and manslaughter, almost 22,000 for rapes, and over 302,000 for aggravated assault. This stands in stark contrast to a total of 81,000 arrests of women for violent offenses. In addition to violent crimes against people, there were more than 186,000 male arrests for vandalism and almost 140,000 arrests for weapons violations.

Many angry men seem proud of the damage that they have done in rage. "I was so mad, I broke my knuckles on the door and didn't even feel it." It's almost as if the injury validates the intensity of the anger, which in turn justifies being out of control. So, you justify the property damage or injuries you inflict by the intensity of your anger. But that is not a valid justification. Simply stated, you are not allowed—you have no right—to aggress against people, property, or yourself just because you are angry. No matter how angry you get.

Victims of Your Violence

There is no excuse for physical aggression. In particular, violence against women or children is inexcusable because they tend to be less physically powerful, less able to defend themselves, and more likely to get hurt. The myths about women enjoying or getting "turned on" by being hit are true only of women who have developed sexual problems, usually through repeated sexual and physical abuse. Women do not need to be shown "who's the boss." They don't "need a good spanking now and then." And women do *not* respect men who hit them.

There is even less justification for hitting a woman than for hitting another man, even if she hits you. As noted above, women are usually smaller and cannot withstand the force of men's attacks. Not only that, they are human beings and deserve respect. Violence against women is an issue of control. First, it is an issue of self-control. You *allow* yourself to get out of control when you hit a woman, because they are safe targets. You wouldn't hit your boss, or a police officer, or a man bigger than yourself (unless you are so out of control that you can't even look out for yourself). They are more dangerous targets and they might hurt you in return. Second, violence is often an issue of attempting to control others. Men use violence in order to control women, to win arguments, to have things their way. Men have no right to exercise this kind of control. Women deserve the same rights, opportunities, and protection from violence as men. When you use violence to "settle" an argument, you are admitting that you have little self-control, that you are too immature to handle it when someone disagrees with you, and that you are, in general, a bully.

146

Angry men also tend to get out of control when they discipline their children. Children have an uncanny ability to frustrate you and push your buttons. But you should be careful how you react to children. In particular, physical punishment of children should be used judiciously, if at all. You should not hit a child in anger. If you think that a child needs to be spanked, it should be done calmly and for a good reason (for example, to stop dangerous behavior, such as playing with fire or running out into the street). Children should not be hit in the head, with objects, or hard enough to leave bruises. Very often, children are spanked because the parent is frustrated, not necessarily because the child's behavior deserved it. "I feared my father. But, by God, I respected him." I'll bet you didn't really respect him and I'll bet even more that you didn't *like* him. And if physical discipline was so good for you, why are you having such trouble with your anger? Is it possible that you were abused yourself and that part of your anger stems from this abuse? In most circumstances, there are disciplinary techniques that are more effective (and much less dangerous) than physical punishment.

A particularly sorry excuse used by many men who abuse children is that they are "preparing them for the real world" or "making them tough." If you were abused as a child, be honest with yourself. Do you *really* think that the abuse made you more capable of handling the real world, more able to control yourself, more happy? What children really need from their parents in order to prepare them for the real world is confidence. Confidence to try more and more things on their own. Confidence to make the transition from childish dependence to mature independence. Abuse does not make confident children. Abuse produces children who are afraid to make a move on their own. Abuse teaches children that if you rock the boat, you will suffer. Abuse makes angry and resentful children who feel helpless to avoid pain.

Physical punishment also damages your relationship with children. When you physically hurt a child, you become associated with the pain. So the sight of you is a signal to the child that he can expect pain and suffering instead of love and other good feelings. Let's use pets as an example. If there is one family member who always hits the dog and one who always feeds the dog, which person is the dog going to fear and avoid? Which person will the dog love and enjoy? It works the same way with children. There are more effective ways than physical discipline to train children and pets.

are you out of control?

Here are seven red flags to let you know that you cannot manage your violent anger...

- You've hit your wife or girlfriend—even just once
- You get into fights with other men
- You hit your children when you are angry
- You damage your or other people's property in anger
- You frequently hit your pets in anger
- You injure yourself in anger (such as by punching things)
- You exhibit "road rage"

Angry men should also remember that children learn a great deal by observation. If you show them that physical aggression is the way to settle problems, they will learn to aggress whenever they face frustration or difficulty in their own lives. You will be helping to create another generation of angry men. "Do as I say, not as I do" is a ridiculous statement. Of course children are going to imitate their parents and other adults, and their parents have a responsibility to demonstrate the types of behavior that they would be proud of in their children. Men who are in control of themselves demonstrate to their children that frustration or difficult times in life can be handled. They teach their children by their good example that when something doesn't work or goes wrong, the thing to do is try another method.

Four Strategies to Avoid Violence

1. "Don't hit. Walk away."

One of the most basic methods for preventing abuse is to leave the frustrating situation, immediately. If you and your wife are having a disagreement and you are beginning to feel out of control, leave the house. Take a walk. Sit outside. Do anything to remove yourself from the source of frustration. However, you should not go for a drive in your car or on your motorcycle. Angry men do not belong on the road when they are that angry.

You may believe that walking away does not solve anything. That the problem is still there, unsolved. But the major problem to be solved before any others is your tendency to strike out when angry. All other problems are less important that this one. And once you cool off, you may find that the original problem is not as important as it felt in the heat of an argument. So, until you learn to control yourself, get yourself away from the situation that is making you angry.

You should also practice saying things to yourself that will help you to remember to get out of the situation when you need to. Dr. Raymond Novaco suggests the following self-talk for this purpose. "Don't hit. Walk away. Don't hit. Walk away. Don't hit. Walk away." Practice saying this to yourself over and over again when you are not angry. Take 10 or 15 minutes every day and repeat this to yourself, over and over and over again. You may feel silly at first. Change is uncomfortable. But, by making this phrase as automatic as possible, you increase the chance that it will pop into your head when you need it.

Avoiding a situation in which you might hit someone is not "chickening out," "backing down," or admitting that you are wrong. It is exercising self-control. You pride yourself on your self-control; here is a chance to exercise some beneficial self-control. Get out before you do something that you will regret later. Later on, you will learn more sophisticated methods for controlling yourself. But for now, avoidance is the key. Don't hit. Walk away.

Be ready for those around you to resist this change. Remember, people are uncomfortable with change. For example, as you try to leave the house before hitting your wife, she may follow you. She may call you a coward, accuse you of refusing to deal with the issue, or find other ways to insult you. Tough it out. Follow through with your plan. Do not let yourself be controlled by your anger. If you persist in avoiding physical violence, your friends, family, and coworkers will get used to your new self-control and will ease up on their attempts to provoke you. Later on, you will develop more sophisticated methods for handling your tendency to get angry and out of control.

2. Exercise

Anger is energy. If you have a problem with physical aggression, you need to get rid of some energy. You may find that regular, intense exercise helps you to expend some of that energy and stay in better control. Aerobic exercise has been found to be a very good treatment for depression, anxiety, and anger. A man who has worn himself out running, swimming, or in an aerobics class has less energy left for angry explosions. (However, boxing or martial arts practice are probably not good ways for the angry man to get exercise!) In addition to the direct benefits for your anger, exercise will tone you up and give you a feeling of control over your life. These side benefits may also be important for your anger control. In addition to the benefits you'll reap from a long-term exercise program, doing something exhausting is a good way to defuse your anger immediately. For example, if you find yourself getting out of control, go run a couple of miles.

Your angry energy can also be expended in other socially acceptable ways. For example, many artists express their anger through their art. Artists who would never assault anyone will sometimes produce very violent artwork. Many writers describe violent acts that they would never carry out themselves. Many psychologists refer to this as *catharsis*, the therapeutic release of anger and other dangerous emotions in non-destructive ways. You may not be an artist, but there are many ways that you can release dangerous energy before it becomes destructive. Competitive sports are one way. Basketball, racquet sports, and running are all competitive forms of intense exercise that may help you to control your angry energy until you get a better handle on avoiding the buildup of anger in the first place. But don't transfer your tendency to fight at home into fights on the basketball court. Just play hard. Releasing your anger in this way will have the added benefit of engaging you in activities that you enjoy, in other words, accepting pleasure.

In addition to physically active ways of managing your anger, you might want to consider more calm and relaxing approaches to anger control. Frustration is a major source of anger for many men. And a big part of frustration for many men comes from feelings of time pressure. Pressure to get things done at work. Pressure to take care of projects around the house. Pressure to be more places and do more things than is humanly possible. You should consider finding ways to relax and unwind on a regular basis. Get a weekly massage. After exercise, sit in a steam bath or sauna for awhile. Go fishing. Ride your motorcycle out into the country. Do your gardening. Schedule time to read a novel. Do something to slow down!

3. Get rid of weapons

Do not keep weapons in your house until you have learned much better anger management skills. Other people may be able to justify possession of guns or other weapons for hunting or self-protection. *The angry man should not keep any weapons in the house for any reason.* A large percentage of deadly assaults with guns are between people who know each other, often spouses, friends, or lovers. Let someone else keep your hunting rifle, shotgun, or handgun until you have gained better control over your temper. You may be saying to yourself that you have just as much of a right as anyone else to have a gun. Of course you have the legal right to keep a gun in your house (if your jurisdiction permits it). But until you get better control over your temper, you should not exercise this right.

4. Avoid alcohol

Avoid alcohol. Remember, alcohol reduces inhibitions. Until you get control over your temper and your tendency to abuse others, you need *more* inhibitions, not fewer. You should never allow yourself to be under the influence of alcohol. Alcohol reduces inhibitions long before you actually feel drunk. "I can hold my liquor." Fine, but don't put yourself to the test.

When to Get Help

If, after reading this chapter, you engage in *any* physical confrontation with your wife, your lover, or other men, you should seek professional assistance immediately.

You will have demonstrated that you cannot control your violent tendencies on your own, even though you are trying your best to do so. If you engage in overly harsh, unreasonable, or frequent physical punishment of your children, see a psychologist or other mental health professional. If you become violent against your pets or your belongings, seriously consider the possibility that you have a problem that, at present, is bigger than you can handle on your own.

Violent behavior can be corrected. But you must attend to it at once, before you hurt yourself or others.

14

FALLING ON YOUR CRUTCH
when substance abuse makes anger worse

One of the worst things that an angry man can do is succumb to the temptations of drug and alcohol abuse. Regardless of your reasons for doing so, the use of drugs—primarily marijuana—or alcohol will not help your anger problems, and there is a very real chance that it will make them worse. Not only that, but you also run the risks of ruining your health, your family life, and your job. And you may wind up in jail or prison.

Many angry men have a problem with drug or alcohol abuse. There are as many reasons for this as there are angry men. Some find that they feel better temporarily when they are under the influence of drugs or alcohol. Others are impulsive and do it without even thinking about why or considering the consequences. Some angry men find that it is easier to be around people when they use drugs or alcohol. And some men use such substances because their subculture supports it—the people they live with use drugs or alcohol, and the angry man has always had access to them. It is possible to "fall into" drug or alcohol abuse when just about everyone you know is doing it.

Many men are not able to stop their drug use, even when they sincerely wish to. Addiction, peer pressure, and poor coping skills will all pull you back into drug use and are difficult to deal with on your own. If you wish to quit using drugs and have not been able to do so on your own, you must get professional help before it is too late.

Alcohol Dependency

Alcohol is probably the most commonly abused drug. Alcohol is a particular problem for men with anger control problems because it escalates the intensity of anger. Alcohol is involved in a large percentage of the violence directed at one's self and at others. According to the National Clearinghouse for Alcohol and Drug Information, alcohol is a "key factor" in 68 percent of manslaughter cases, 62 percent of assaults, and 54 percent of murders and attempted murders. Among prison inmates, 42 percent of those convicted of rape reported being under the influence of alcohol at the time of the offense. Alcohol is a factor in more than 50 percent of incidents of domestic violence. It is also a significant factor in most suicides.

One of the main links between alcohol and anger is its tendency to lower the drinker's inhibitions. This is the reason that people use alcohol to "loosen up" socially. Alcohol makes it easier for people to relax, talk to other people, "get rowdy," and do what they feel like doing without worrying about what other people think. This leads to dancing on tabletops, indiscriminate sexual liaisons, and other behaviors that people would normally suppress or inhibit.

Since the "free love" period of the 1960s, being inhibited or "uptight" has been thought of as a bad thing. People are told to "loosen up" and go with their feelings. But not all inhibitions are bad. If we are going to live around other people, we have to inhibit many of our basic impulses. Just because we feel like having sex with our best friend's wife, this doesn't mean we should do it. Just because you want to shoplift a soda doesn't mean that you should do it. And just because someone makes you mad doesn't mean that you should act on your impulse to hit him.

By reducing our inhibitions, alcohol can fan the flames of anger. Angry men who drink alcohol usually get angry more often, more intensely, and with less provocation than if alcohol were not in their systems. When an angry man drinks alcohol, not only is he more easily provoked, but he is also more likely to get physical with his anger. Alcohol can turn a discussion into a disagreement, a disagreement into an argument, an argument into a fight, or a fight into an all-out assault. Angry men should avoid alcohol or at least reduce their consumption. As we all know, it is very difficult for people to get back into control of their drinking once a pattern of alcohol abuse has begun. Alcohol abusers are

are you abusing alcohol?

Any of the following indicates an alcohol problem:
- Driving while under the influence (whether or not you get caught)
- Injuries suffered when drunk (for example, from falls)
- Physical disease (such as liver or brain disease)
- Fighting, loss of friends
- Restricted social life (for example, avoiding church activities or party invitations)
- Deterioration of your family life (such as estrangement from your wife or children)
- Hangovers that interfere with work
- Drinking on the job
- Injuries to others caused by your drinking, whether deliberately or accidentally

also abusers of denial. They find many childish ways to convince themselves that they are not abusing alcohol. They go to extreme lengths to hide their abuse from themselves and others. But if you are going to eliminate alcohol as a factor in your anger, you have to be honest with yourself about the problem. You know you are abusing alcohol if you are damaging your health, your social life, your family life, or your job or if you are placing others at risk when you drink.

You also know you've got a problem if you've tried to quit or cut down and haven't been able to do it, tried to control your drinking by limiting the amount, times, or places of drinking, or find yourself defending your drinking to yourself.

This is not a complete list of symptoms of problem drinking, but if any of these sound familiar to you, you should be honest with yourself and determine whether or not you have a problem.

When to Get Help
Some people can control their problem drinking on their own. Many cannot. If you think you need professional assistance, you should take steps to get it. Chapters of Alcoholics Anonymous are available in most

communities in the United States. Psychologists, psychiatrists, social workers, and certified alcohol counselors are also available. If you decide to get professional assistance with your alcohol problem, be sure to ask the professional whether he or she is specifically trained in the treatment of alcohol abuse.

Marijuana Abuse

Many angry men like the effects of marijuana. Marijuana helps these men to "chill out." It can produce a feeling of relaxation, mellowness, and amiability—exactly the feelings that angry men are missing in their lives. It may be that the only way that you can relax and not worry, or feel happy and at ease, is to smoke marijuana. If so, you might want to consider getting professional help to find other ways to obtain these same feelings. Because marijuana can interfere with your life as well. Although marijuana does not seem to produce nearly the level of damage to your body that alcohol does, it can interfere with your life in many ways. Trying to study for school, concentrate on your work, or deal with a crisis are next to impossible when you are stoned. Marijuana impairs your memory while you are under the influence. So if you try to learn anything while you are stoned, it will take you longer and you won't learn it as well.

As far as your anger goes, marijuana's effects are paradoxical. On the one hand, it helps you stay calm. On the other hand, it prevents you from learning how to control yourself on your own. If you get stoned every time you feel "stressed out," you will never learn to handle stress on your own. What happens when you have to deal with a stressful event and you can't get stoned? If you smoke a joint every night when you get home from work, how can your relationships with your family ever deepen? As you begin to take more and more control over your anger, you must continually ask yourself if you are asking marijuana to do things for you that you would rather be able to do for yourself. If so, it's best to quit the marijuana and put the lessons in Part Two to use.

15

ANGER TURNED INWARD
depression's grim effects on angry men

According to the National Institute of Mental Health, more than 19 million people suffer from depressive illnesses. In my clinical experience, most of my angry patients have depression in one form or another. Sigmund Freud believed that depression was "anger turned inward." From the perspective of a clinical psychologist, it is hard to argue against this notion because so many of the symptoms of depression seem to be forms of self-punishment. Depressed people do not enjoy much of anything that they do. They don't have any energy, can't sleep, and don't want to be around people. Depressed people often don't enjoy their food and have no interest in sex. And depressed people often punish themselves in a more permanent way, by killing themselves.

But on a more immediate level, depression may be contributing to your anger. We are used to thinking of depression as a *mood*. But depression is not a mood. It is a disorder, and depressed mood is only one symptom of it. If you are depressed, you may not actually feel sad, down in the dumps, blue, or depressed. Rather, if you are like many angry men, when you get depressed, it may make you feel irritable and angry. Depression reduces your tolerance, patience, and self-confidence to even lower levels than usual, and this can lead to even more anger. Little annoyances seem like major catastrophes. The noise of children playing feels like it is taking place inside your skull. Any demands made upon you at work or at home seem overwhelming.

The Causes of Depression

No one really knows what causes depression, although scientists from many disciplines have learned a tremendous amount in the past 20 years. We know that depression runs in families. So, as with many other behavioral and physical traits, there is probably a genetic predisposition to depression. But the precise way that this occurs is still not known. We are also pretty sure that brain chemistry is involved in some way and modern anti-depressant medications seem to do their job by manipulating serotonin and other chemicals. The fact that depression often strikes for no particular reason again supports the notion that something internal is going on.

But we also know that environmental factors contribute to depression. The simplest example that illustrates this is grieving over the death of a loved one or suffering through the breakup of a marriage. People can become depressed due to stressful events in their lives. Whether or not biologically based, or *endogenous*, depressive episodes are different from externally caused, or *exogenous*, episodes is still a matter of intense debate and research.

The Experience of Depression

But this issue is probably not really important for your situation. It doesn't matter why you are depressed; it still hurts and it still contributes to your anger. And it still may need some intense work before it will go away.

Recent research is investigating the possibility that some people experience "anger attacks" much the same way that others experience anxiety attacks. These anger attacks involve sudden outbursts of anger that may be uncharacteristic for that person, are inappropriate for the situation, and involve physical features such as sweating, trembling, increased heart rate, and hot flashes. Not only that, but anger attacks are thought to be much more common in depressed people than in those who do not suffer from depression. In fact, researchers currently estimate that 30 to 40 percent of depressed patients will experience anger attacks. The good news is that treatment with modern antidepressants seems to help reduce or eliminate these outbursts.

are you depressed?

Major depressive episodes can be recognized by the following symptoms:

- Depressed (or irritable) mood
- Significant weight gain or loss
- Either insomnia or sleeping too much
- Fatigue and loss of energy
- Feelings of worthlessness or inappropriate guilt
- Difficulty concentrating or making decisions
- Loss of interest or pleasure in activities (including sex)
- Thoughts of death or suicide, and suicide attempts

Depressed and angry men tend to isolate themselves. The effort of making conversation, being polite, and looking interested are exhausting to a depressed man. When you are depressed, you just want to be left alone! So you avoid people whenever possible. But this can lead to a cycle that can make you even more depressed. Even though it is completely illogical, when your depression leads you to isolate yourself, you can end up feeling neglected and unwanted. Even though it is *you* who are avoiding people, it feels like they are avoiding you. And again, even though the whole cycle is not logical, when you feel unwanted or unfairly treated, you will feel more depressed and angry.

Depression will give you a negative and pessimistic outlook on life. When you are depressed, you cannot see anything but doom and gloom. The psychologist Aaron Beck has described a "cognitive triad" that sums up the thoughts of depressed individuals. Depressed people tend to believe that "I'm worthless. The world is worthless. And there is no hope for change or improvement." For depressed people, the glass is always half empty. You probably recognize this type of thinking from our earlier discussions of how the angry man sees himself and the world. Angry men tend to focus on the worst and to have an irrationally low opinion of themselves. So, we start out with an angry man who probably already has very few positive things to say about himself, and then he gets depressed. The depression makes his thinking even more negative. Let's add to this mix another characteristic of depression: feelings of guilt for no good reason. What a combination for more anger!

Depressed people find ways to make themselves guilty for every bad thing that happens around them. If you already carry around too much guilt, as many angry men do, the added guilt burden of a depressive episode can make you feel absolutely without value.

Depression is not necessarily something that is with you all the time. Most people who suffer from depression will have periodic major depressive episodes. These episodes may last for days, weeks, or even months. But they eventually subside, and the person may feel relatively normal until the next episode.

Everyone experiences *some* of these symptoms *some* of the time. But if more than half of them pertain to you or if you feel this way for days, weeks, or months at a time, you are probably suffering from depression. Most depressed individuals will not exhibit all of these characteristics. But if you see several of these in yourself, you may be depressed. Just because you don't feel this way all of the time, it does not mean that you do not suffer from depression. For most depressed people, periods of depression alternate with periods of relative normality. Angry men, unfortunately, tend to deny their depression once an episode begins to subside. This leads to another common cycle that we see in psychiatry and psychology—people seek treatment only when they are depressed, and they stop treatment as soon as it helps them feel a little bit better. The depression inevitably returns, and we begin the cycle anew.

Depression can reduce your morale and productivity at work. It can take all the joy out of your family life. Depression can ruin your sex drive and make even this pleasurable activity seem like a chore. Depression can make it hard for you to concentrate. When an angry man becomes depressed, he has even less tolerance for frustration than he did before, again leading to more anger.

Bipolar Depression

Another type of mood disorder can fire up your anger. This disorder is known as *bipolar depression* or *manic depression*. Bipolar depression has

are you bipolar?

The manic episodes are characterized by the following signs:

- Energized mood. This mood change can be either euphoric or irritable.
- Inflated self-esteem and an unreasonably high opinion of yourself.
- Decreased need for sleep
- Excessive talkativeness
- Racing thoughts
- Distractibility
- Restlessness and a need to keep moving
- Intense goal-directed activity
- Impulsivity (manifest in such behaviors as spending sprees, sexual promiscuity, or foolish investments)

three primary characteristics: depressive episodes (which we just learned about), manic episodes, and general impulsivity. Persons suffering from bipolar depression will usually have separate depressive and manic episodes that are interspersed with periods of relative normality. As with depression, the causes of bipolar depression are not exactly known. But it seems to have an even stronger genetic basis than regular, or unipolar, depression.

Many people who have never experienced a manic episode imagine that they are fun. And although many people suffering manic episodes have fun for awhile, the euphoria is generally short-lived. It is more likely that they feel irritable and agitated. Their anger is easily provoked. People in the middle of a manic episode feel like they are about to jump out of their skin.

While the mood swings that people with bipolar disorder experience are unpleasant, it is impulsivity that gets such people into trouble. Impulsivity is a tendency to act without considering the consequences of your actions. Examples of impulsive behavior include shoplifting, sexual promiscuity, drug or alcohol abuse, poor money management (such as risky investments or spending sprees), extramarital affairs, suicide attempts, or thrill-seeking, such as racing with other drivers or taking dares. Impulsive people are also prone to emotional outbursts, including tears, rage, or euphoria. Persons with bipolar disorder tend to make their decisions based upon how they feel rather than by being more logical and analytical about their choices. When your primary justification for your behavior is that you "felt like it," you are usually headed for trouble. Bipolar patients tend to have difficulty in most areas of their lives. They get into trouble with the law, have a hard time staying in a marriage, and don't manage their work lives all that well. Other people have extreme difficulty putting up with the volatile moods and unpredictable behavior.

Not all people who are suffering from bipolar disorder will experience manic episodes, but many do. If you experience depressive episodes and seem to always be doing things that you regret later, you may be suffering from bipolar depression. If you do suffer from this disorder, you will probably have an even greater tendency to lose control of your anger.

How to Get Help

Depression and bipolar depression are serious psychological problems for which you should seek professional attention. Psychiatric help in the form of anti-depressant medication is available. Psychological help is available in the form of psychological therapy. Admitting that you may be depressed does not mean that you are "crazy," "mentally ill," or having a "nervous breakdown." It also does not mean that you are weak, unmanly, or that you "can't handle" your life. Depressed individuals simply have more to contend with than others do, and professionally trained mental health experts can make the process of coping easier. You may be able to get by on your own without help, but it could very well be easier *with* help. And you may spend more of your time feeling upbeat and being productive if you let trained professionals give you a hand.

Several types of antidepressant medications have shown promise in reducing the severity of depression. Until the past several years, the most common type of antidepressant medications in use was tricyclic antidepressants. These include medications such as Elavil, Pamelor, Norpramin, Anafranil, Sinequan, Tofranil, and Desyrel. Another class of antidepressants, known as monoamine oxidase inhibitors (MAOIs), include Nardil and Parnate. More recently, a new class of antidepressants has been developed. These are known as selective serotonin reuptake inhibitors (SSRIs) and include such medications as Prozac, Zoloft, and Paxil. Other medications are particularly effective for bipolar depression; these include Calan, Depakote, Tegretol, and various forms of lithium.

Your psychiatrist may suggest one of these medications to you, depending on the characteristics of your depression, your age, and other life circumstances. Don't be discouraged if you do not notice an immediate improvement in your mood. Most antidepressants need two to three weeks to have an effect, since it takes this long for your body to build up a therapeutic blood level of the medication. Even if you do not feel any difference after several weeks, be patient. The particular medication that you are taking may not be effective for you, or the dose may need to be altered. Your psychiatrist may decide to try a different medication if you continue to show little or no improvement.

Prescribing anti-depressants is not like treating an infection with an antibiotic. It may take several months of trial and error to get the right medication and the right dose for you. On the other hand, you may get good results right off the bat. But be patient—this will be good practice for you!

As with any chemical that goes into your body, your antidepressant medication may produce side effects. These are unwanted physical or psychological reactions to the medication in addition to the beneficial or "therapeutic" effects. Some of the more common side effects of antidepressant medications are sleep disturbances, dry mouth, constipation, weight gain or loss, and loss of sex drive. You should not automatically discontinue your medication if you experience side effects; many of them are temporary. Above all, *you should not discontinue your medication or alter your dose without consulting your psychiatrist.* Together, you and your psychiatrist should decide if the beneficial effects outweigh the side effects. It is also important to remember that you must take your antidepressant medications as prescribed in order for them to be effective. If you only take them when you feel depressed, they will not work. Remember, it is necessary to keep a constant, therapeutic blood level in order for your medication to work for you.

"I don't want to get hooked." "I don't like to take any medicine; I don't even take aspirin." "I don't want to be dependent on medicine; I want to do it myself." "I don't want to be a zombie." Angry men have many "reasons" not to try anti-depressant medication. Most of them are superficial. Would you take an antibiotic for a sinus infection? Would you take insulin for diabetes? Would you take an anti-hypertensive medication for your high blood pressure? Of course you would (if you've got any sense)! Then why do you think that you should be able to treat the most complex organ in your body—your brain—with no help? Antidepressant medication is not addictive. These drugs are not abusable in the way that street drugs are because there is no immediate, significant change in the way that you feel. In other words, you will not get "high" or get a "rush." It is also unlikely that you will feel like a "zombie." Many of the old antipsychotic drugs sometimes had this effect, especially when they were prescribed inappropriately. But it is unusual for an antidepressant to make you feel this way. If you do get some side effects, like lethargy or fatigue, simply tell your psychiatrist and the two of you, working together as a team, will decide what to do about it. Also, there is no reason why you will not be able to decrease the dose or stop taking the drug at some point in the future. But again, this must be done in consultation with your psychiatrist. More important, though, the "I don't need the medication" attitude is probably another example of the angry man's tendency to refuse to accept the help that is available. Take advantage of what 21st-century science has to offer you.

Beyond Medication

For most angry men, depression is related to how they view themselves and the world. Many of the characteristics of angry men that we have described—for example, pessimism—are exacerbated by depression. Similarly, depression can kill your motivation to achieve and can contribute to your low opinion of yourself. If low tolerance for frustration, stress, and any disagreement with others is part of your anger, depression will make these tendencies of yours even worse. While medication may take much of the pain out of a depressive episode (and prevent others from occurring in the future), you still need to learn different ways of thinking and different ways of interacting with those around you. A counselor or psychologist can help you to do this. In fact, research shows that, at 12 months after treatment, therapy and medication are usually equally effective—and the best outcome is achieved if antidepressants are used concurrently with professional therapy. In addition, the simple fact of talking to an understanding and objective person about depression feels good to many angry men. Many, many angry men brood about our problems, go around and around with themselves about their "guilt," their "fault," and "what I should have done." They drive themselves crazy with this useless crap. The objective observations and suggestions of another person, especially a trained person who truly cares about how you feel, can help you focus in on what's truly important. Once you learn to focus your brain, you can focus on your goals for changing your behavior. This will help you to make changes in your life that will reduce the crap and help you to feel less angry.

PART FOUR

anger-free families

Almost all of the angry men who enter my office tell me stories about the crud in their family lives that has contributed to their anger. Why do so many angry men feel as though their formative years were so awful? Why do so many families produce so many angry men?

Anger is not only an individual trait but is also a characteristic of families. Angry men tend to have angry fathers, brothers, grandfathers, and uncles (as well as angry mothers, sisters, grandmothers, and aunts). Anger gets passed from one generation to the next, and if you are to do something about your own anger, you will have to come to terms with the part that your relationships with your family play in the history of your anger and its continuation. You will have to identify the things about your family that are fueling your anger and somehow get those things out of your life. And you'll have to learn how to end the cycle of anger in your own family—especially with your own sons. The women in your family will have to help, too. You'll find strategies for ending the family legacy of anger in the following chapters. There is also a chapter for the women who are reading this book in order to help them understand the angry men in their lives.

16

GOING HOME AGAIN
learning to leave your anger behind

How does anger get passed from one generation to the next? Why do angry fathers breed angry sons? Why do so many angry men have so much resentment toward their families? Much of what we learn as children comes from our parents and family. If we see that our parents react to frustration by getting angry, that is what we learn to do. If we hear story after story about the things that our fathers and uncles did when they were angry, we accept this as the way to be. We all want to emulate our elders. Violent crime also tends to run in families. If their elders are always on the attack, boys will do so too. So, one of the reasons that anger runs in families is that we learn how to be angry by watching our angry parents.

The second way that anger runs in families is when angry adults abuse their children (see Chapter 18, "Like Father, Like Son"). Physical abuse, verbal abuse, humiliation, and belittling all contribute to a child's development of anger. Angry adults tend to vent their anger on those who are powerless to do anything about it. They punish out of anger instead of for teaching purposes. When children learn that they will be physically or psychologically hurt and there is nothing that they can do about it, a silent rage begins. Soon that silent rage is no longer silent, and we have produced another angry man. You can see this in the legacy of abuse. Men who abuse their wives and children tend to have been abused themselves or to have watched their mothers be abused by the men in their lives.

171

As I have discussed before, alcohol fans the flames of anger. When it comes to families, there is a strong tendency from generation to generation to abuse alcohol. Thus, a third, indirect way that anger gets passed from one generation to the next is by passing along the family pattern of alcohol abuse.

There are probably both genetic and environmental reasons for the family patterns of anger in the world. But even if we don't know exactly why anger runs in families, there are things that you do about your own anger and the complicated family influences that produced your anger and also serve to keep it festering.

Get Some Distance

The first thing that many angry men have to do is put some distance between themselves and their family. If it seems that everyone in your family knows too much about your business and this makes you angry, take your business somewhere else. Rather than living in your family's home or neighborhood, or even in the same city, you may need to get away. Many men complain that their families are all trying to tell them how to run their lives. They criticize the way they raise their kids, run their businesses, even wear their clothes. If this is one of the things about your family that makes you angry, go somewhere where they won't all be watching you every second of every day.

There may be some costs associated with this move, however. Your parents won't be there to baby-sit your kids for you. Your brother won't be able to help you paint your house. You may miss out on some of the family get-togethers. But for every benefit in life, there are associated costs. If the costs of your family's intrusion in your life outweigh the benefits that you get from being around them, get some distance. Otherwise, you may just have to learn to cope with their intrusiveness.

Change the Script

Families are systems, and every family member has a role to play in that family system. And systems do not like to change. It is therefore going to be hard for you to get out of your old role in your family. If you were always getting in trouble and were the family scapegoat, your family will tend to continue to blame you for everything even when you are grown. If you were the oldest and were expected to keep all of your brothers and sisters in line, you will also be expected to be the leader when you become an adult.

Many of the family roles that we fall into as children and continue into adulthood can be very potent sources of our anger. Did it always make you mad when your know-it-all big brother told you every move to make as a child? Is he still doing it now that you are both adults? It still makes you mad, doesn't it? It makes you feel as though no one believes that you can do anything right or make even the simplest decision for yourself. Did your mother rely on humiliation to try to keep you in line? Chances are your interactions with her still fall into the old, maddening pattern. "You should be ashamed of yourself for the way you treat me. All I asked was for you to take me out every now and then." "Everything was fine until you got married. Now you don't even visit your own mother." Sound familiar?

You can refuse to continue to play out the roles that you have always had in your family. If you don't want your brother telling you what to do, don't discuss your decisions with him. If mealtimes or holidays were always unpleasant, angry times at your house, don't spend these times at your family home. If you feel taken advantage of because your brothers and sisters rely on you to take care of your parents, don't volunteer to do it all the time. You can choose to change the ways that you interact with your family.

Make a list of the things involving your family that most reliably make you angry. Do you always seem to get angry during Sunday dinner at your parents' home? Does everyone's advice on investments make you feel stupid and angry? Does your mother call you too much? You will probably be able to come with two or three things right off the top of your head. When you have made your list, make another list of the commonsense changes that you can make in your behavior to reduce the anger-producing impact of these things. Don't make the mistake of waiting for your family to change *their* behavior. They won't. Don't let yourself fall into the trap of thinking "Why should I have to do all the changing?" You have to take responsibility for your own happiness within your family and make the changes from your end.

Cover Up Your Buttons

No one knows your sensitive issues, your "hot buttons," better than your family. After all, they were the ones pushing them for all those years! For most of us, the issues that angered us as children and teens are similar to the issues that anger us now. "Remember when you..." is a sure-fire lead-in to an argument that you had years ago, and probably more than once. Don't have it again. Did a particular nickname enrage you as a child? It will probably still make you mad as an adult.

Your hot buttons will usually be related to the parts of your life that you are insecure about. Maybe you never thought that you were very good-looking and spent lots of time in the bathroom when you were getting ready to go out. It is still going to make you angry when your family makes jokes about standing in line waiting for you to pinch your zits. But when you look at it dispassionately, is it anything to get concerned about now? You probably don't even have zits now! The point is that if you want to be more relaxed and less provoked around your family, it will help if you sit down and think about the things that they say and do that can always get a rise out of you. After you have done this, decide how you will handle yourself the next time they bring them up. One method is to beat them to the punch. As soon as someone begins telling the same old annoying story again, break in and finish the story for them. This takes the wind out of their sails and puts you in charge of the situation. If you can do this with a bit of humor, even better. Maybe the story is funny. If you can laugh at it too, you are doing a good job of eliminating one source of anger from your life.

Another way to handle the situation is to say nothing. Remember, they are only reminding you of this part of your past because it gets a rise out of you. If you can sit there like nothing happened, the impact of the story is virtually nil. The bottom line is that you should anticipate the buttons that your family is likely to push and cover them up!

Put an End to Feuds

Family members have a way of making mountains out of molehills. Little disagreements result in brothers and sisters, or parents and children, not speaking to each other. No one is willing to make the first move and the silent treatment can go on for years, long after the original issue has been forgotten. Even when both family members would rather return to a normal relationship, each is afraid to make the first move. Are you afraid to make the first move because you fear that you will be rejected and that this will be embarrassing?

If you want your feuds to come to an end, don't wait for your brother to make up to you. Take control of your own life and happiness and make the first move. It's not so much a matter of swallowing your pride as much as it is overcoming your discomfort. Your brother may tell you to get lost. You have no control over his behavior. But chances are that he is just as unhappy with the feud as you are and will respond positively.

On the other hand, there may be some members of your family that you will never get along with. No one ever said that you have to like your family. They are people just like any others. Some you will like and some you will not. While you do have certain responsibilities toward your family, it is up to you to decide how much interaction you want to have with them.

Support the Next Generation

Nothing is more disheartening than seeing the family garbage being passed to the next generation. It will hit you like a ton of bricks when your son or niece says something that sounds strangely like something you said when you were that age. And you will understand how unhappy that child is. When they act as you acted when you were miserable, you will know that they are headed down the same road you've been down unless something changes. Your ability to make things better for them is limited. But you are not totally powerless.

Take an interest in the youngsters. Maybe they need a favorite uncle to talk to every now and then. Maybe they need someone they can call when their car breaks down. Maybe they need some financial help from time to time. What they really need is for the adults in their lives to guide them, to show them how to grow up happy. They need to know that they are fundamentally good people. Two of the most important things that you can give children are the feelings of competence and confidence. Don't stand by and do nothing out of fear that you will be seen as nosy or interfering by other family members; make your move. If the other adults tell you to mind your own business after you have tried to help the kids, decide whether or not you should butt out and then follow your conscience.

Rethinking Family

Your family can be a source of strength, confidence, warmth, and love. But it can only be so on your terms. You have to learn how much of you family you need and how you can best have relationships with your family without getting constantly angry. But again, don't wait for them to make those decisions for you. And don't fail to act when you know what to do.

This process will not happen quickly or easily. You may not feel comfortable around certain members of your family for years. And with some, you may never have the kind of relationship you want. They have their issues, too. Maybe they are wrestling with how much of *you* they want in their lives. But if you never try, you will never know.

17

LOVE WITHOUT WAR
making peace with your partner

Earlier in the book, I discussed the impact your anger has on your relationships with women. If you are like most men, you want a happy relationship with a woman. But if you do not learn to deal with women differently, you will never achieve such a relationship. You will have to loosen up your controls, learn to talk more about your feelings, learn to listen when she speaks, and learn to really hear what she is saying. It will also require that you approach your sexual relationships differently.

Just about every angry man that walks into my office sooner or later wants to talk about his dissatisfaction with his sex life. Whether it has to do with the frequency of sex, getting some spice into his sex life, or feeling that his partner does not appreciate him sexually, angry men often don't feel that their needs are getting met. Angry men tend to be very sensitive about the quality of their sex lives. If any little thing does not seem "right," they often feel devastated.

Pressure to Perform

If you're like many angry men, you believe that if a woman does not have an orgasm, there is something wrong with you or your "performance." You worry that your orgasm came too soon, that your technique was bad, or that your penis was too small. It may in fact be the case that you could stand to learn a little bit about sexual technique. But it is likely that there are some distortions in your thinking about sex, based on a lack of knowledge. While an extended discussion of sexual problems and sex therapy is beyond the scope of this book, here are some of the common misconceptions about sex and some suggestions for changing your approach to sex.

First, most women can enjoy sexual intercourse without always having an orgasm. Although there are wide individual differences among women, in general, an orgasm is not as imperative for enjoyment as it is for most men. Because intercourse without orgasm is not fulfilling for most men, men often don't understand how women can enjoy sex without orgasm. But women are different. Ask your partner about this, and listen to what she says.

Second, many women need direct clitoral stimulation (either oral or manual) in order to achieve orgasm. While women certainly do enjoy intercourse, many will not have an orgasm during intercourse regardless of how big your penis is or how long you last. It is a basic fact of female sexual physiology. Take the time to learn what your partner wants.

You will not be doing your sex life any good by making your partner's orgasm something that you do for your own needs and ego rather than something you do for her because she enjoys and desires it. A woman's orgasm is not a measure of your manhood. It is not something that should cause you anxiety. Rather, it is one aspect of your enjoyment of your partner and something that you try to do for her, if and when she would like it.

Don't be afraid to ask your partner what she likes. Men have somehow gotten the idea that they are supposed to know all about the sexual desires of their partners without asking. Well, you don't, and this is a form of mind-reading. Women's wants, needs, and desires are individual, and the only way to know what they are is to ask. For many angry men, it is embarrassing to talk to their partners about sex. But as with any other behavior change, if you can tough it out a few times, it will get easier.

Don't wait until you are upset to talk about your sexual relationship with your partner. If you try to talk about this sensitive topic when you are frustrated or angry, the discussion may very well deteriorate into an argument. It is much better to talk about your sex life when you are calm, maybe even when you are in a good mood. After all, sex is supposed to be fun. Be explicit with her about what turns you on and what you like and don't like. But realize that your partner also has wants and needs. You should be assertive about getting your own needs met and generous about fulfilling your partner's desires as well.

Many angry men try to make up for dissatisfaction and unhappiness in other areas of life by expecting too much from their sex lives. Maybe you've got a crummy job, disrespectful kids, and a bald head. Many angry men come to believe, at least implicitly, that sex should be frequent (perhaps every day) and that every episode should be incredibly exciting and leave the couple semi-conscious with bliss. It's not like that! Just like everything else in your life, sometimes sex is great and sometimes it is mediocre. This is not to say that your sex life cannot be a very satisfying and exciting part of your life. But, you should not place all of your emotional eggs in this one basket. How long would you enjoy your favorite food if you had it for dinner every night? If sex is the only area of your life that is giving any happiness or satisfaction, you need to work on other sources of fun and fulfillment.

It is also important not to get too hung up on what is "normal" in your sex life. Sex between consenting adults enjoys a wide range of normal. This is especially true for frequency of intercourse. Whatever is pleasing and satisfying to the couple is normal for that couple. If one or both members are not satisfied, then you need to talk about what needs to change and try to change it. As in most other areas of your relationship, compromise will be important.

Angry men are very sensitive to rejection, especially when it comes to sex. When a woman indicates that she is not in the mood for sex, it is not necessarily a rejection of the man as a person. In other words, "I don't feel like it tonight, honey" is not the same thing as "I am not attracted to you," "There is something wrong with you," or "You are not a worthwhile person." Frequently, angry men feel rejected because their partners rarely initiate sex. Maybe they never get a chance! If you are initiating sex every day, how would your partner ever get the chance to get horny and approach you first?

Your sex life will be much more satisfying to you if you try to place less emphasis upon frequency and orgasms and more upon having fun and communicating your feelings to your partner. At first, you will certainly feel uncomfortable communicating your feelings about these issues. We already know that such talk makes you nervous. Tough it out. It will get easier with practice!

When to Get Help

As with physical violence, drug or alcohol abuse, and depression, you may find that despite sincere and valiant attempts on your part, you continue to be unhappy with the role of sex in your life. And if you are unhappy about something as important as your sex life, chances are it is continuing to contribute to your anger.

If your partner's orgasm continues to be an issue in your relationship, either for you or for her, you may want to consider getting therapy together. It may be that your partner is also reluctant to talk about her wants and needs. This will make it even more difficult for you to satisfy her. Maybe you could use some suggestions on your technique. Why not take some hints from an expert?

What you want to avoid is letting sex become a source of anxiety rather than a source of excitement, comfort, and love. If you are experiencing long-standing problems in your sex life, the anxiety can lead to problems with your erections. Then the embarrassment of the erectile problems leads some men to avoid sex altogether. This can add to your frustration and anger. While no man is immune from occasional erectile problems, if it happens often, you should get some professional advice.

Other men feel the need to "prove" themselves by "screwing" as many women as possible. For other men, promiscuous sex represents an attempt to get some enjoyment out of an otherwise bleak life. Not only is this extremely risky in these days of serious sexually transmitted diseases, but it is generally a fruitless quest. If you are one of these men, your need to prove yourself will not be fulfilled by repeated empty sex. This is because your problems probably have little to do with sex. Your need for sexual conquest may be an indication that your self-confidence and esteem are generally low. You are trying to patch up your insecurity by reassuring yourself of your manhood. If this is your primary way of getting some enjoyment out of life, you will continue to be frustrated and unhappy. Again, your problems in this area may be more than you can handle on your own, and professional help may be advisable.

Many of the men who get into trouble in their marriages call for an appointment with a psychologist to treat their "sexual addiction." Almost always, they have gotten caught in an extramarital affair. Often, they are also frequent users of pornography and spend time in topless bars. Make no mistake—there is no such thing as sexual addiction.

Rather, the term has been borrowed from the field of drug and alcohol addictions to deflect responsibility from the sexually irresponsible man. If you claim to have a sexual addiction, what you are really trying to do is say "It's not my fault" or "I'm not responsible." Well, you *are* responsible. You choose when and with whom you have sex, and your choices are not due to an addiction.

That is not to say that men do not become obsessed with sex. They do. They will spend inordinate amounts of time, money, and effort seeking out voyeuristic sexual gratification, usually in the form of pornography. This has become very easy with the advent of the Internet and widespread availability of X-rated videotapes. Unfortunately, there is no black-and-white line delineating when someone is spending too much effort in viewing sexual activity. Many individuals and couples find that viewing erotica enhances their sex lives. But if your need to use this material interferes with your relationships or occupies too much of your brain time, it is a problem.

Extramarital affairs are wrong. They are wrong because they are dishonest. They violate your marriage promises and they always involve deception of your wife. There is nothing that justifies this type of deception.

If you are not married and are leading a promiscuous lifestyle, the issues are a bit different. Freud made a distinction between the phallic and genital stages of development. Freud believed that a man who becomes "fixated" at the phallic stage tends to see sex in exploitative terms. The focus is solely on pleasing himself. There is little in the way of mature emotional intercourse with a woman. The genital stage was described by Freud as the attainment of the ability to have a mature and reciprocal emotional commitment with a woman in which sex is a vehicle for the exchange of pleasure unselfishly, as well as to communicate feelings to your partner. While we may not agree with much of what Freud had to say, this distinction is informative.

You cannot dismiss irresponsible sexual behavior by saying you have an addiction. You are responsible for your behavior and you *can* control yourself. Again, though, you may need professional help.

You have an even a more severe problem if you are one of those men who will not take "no" for an answer when it comes to sex. If you have ever forced a woman into sexual acts that she did not wish to be involved in, you have serious problems that need immediate professional attention. There are some lines that can *never* be crossed, and this is one of them. There is no question here. If you have sexually assaulted a woman, you must get professional attention immediately.

Life Isn't All about Sex

But I am violating my own rule by placing too much emphasis on sex! There are many more issues between angry men and women that need to be straightened out. In particular, you have got to quit trying to control every move your wife or girlfriend makes. There is a simple rule here. She is allowed—she has the right—to do everything that you are allowed to do! She is allowed to have opinions. She is allowed to have a career. She is allowed to spend money. She is allowed to go out with friends. She is allowed to participate on an equal basis in the decisions that are made with regard to your finances, vacation plans, meal menus, and so on. She is allowed to pick her own clothes, choose her makeup style, talk to people, spend time with her family, and decide when and if she has sex and when and if she has children.

You will have to make sacrifices in your career to accommodate hers, just as you have expected her to do for your career. You will have to share the housework and the childcare. You will have to stay home from work with sick kids sometimes and take them to soccer practice or piano lessons. You can no longer expect to direct every aspect of your wife's or girlfriend's life and treat her like (poorly) paid help.

When you relax the controls, you may begin to feel jealous. Your wife may achieve more than you. People may listen to what she has to say. Men may look at her. She may be asked to do things that do not include you. Your jealousy is not an indication of your love. It is an indication of your lack of self-confidence. You must keep your jealous thoughts to yourself and go back to the exercises suggested in Part Two of this book in order to change them.

The bottom line here is respect. If you are going to have a mutually satisfying life with a woman, you must learn to respect her and accord her the same rights and privileges that you would want for yourself.

18

LIKE FATHER, LIKE SON
freeing your boy from the grip of anger

Your anger didn't appear suddenly, without warning. You did not go to bed one night carefree and wake up the next morning in a permanent rage. Before you became an angry man, you were probably an angry boy. Sometimes men can point to a single traumatic event or period in their childhoods that produced dramatic changes in their outlook. It's more likely, though, that your anger developed over time, just like your muscles, your intelligence, and your talents.

Can you look back and honestly say that you had a happy childhood? Are most of your memories good ones? Did you have close friends? Did you enjoy school?

Or did it seem that someone was always yelling at you? Do you remember feeling like nobody cared about you? Do you feel a lot of guilt about things that you did as a child? You may not have recognized it at the time, but as you look back, it is possible that you were already angry when you were a boy.

While there are certainly biological predispositions to behavioral and emotional characteristics, a child's experiences while growing up have a huge influence on the person he will become. Even though we say that many boys are a "chip off the old block," don't think that boys are born angry, destined to be angry all of their lives. Angry boys are created by improper treatment and unhealthy home situations. Children need to be nurtured and tended, both physically and emotionally. Many are not. And for many, the result of poor nurturing is chronic anger.

Sal was raised in a large, working-class family in Detroit. His parents argued with each other and with their own brothers and sisters. It was not unusual for dinner to be interrupted by a raging argument among the adults at the table. The arguments were profane, insulting, and often ended up with food thrown around the room or physical fights in the yard. If Sal got out of line, a chorus of abuse was in store for him, often followed by a slap to the back of the head.

At Thanksgiving in the year Sal turned 10 years, the entire extended family was at Sal's house for dinner. He had written a poem in class that week and he wanted to read it before dinner. He stood up to read and had barely gotten through the first line when the catcalls started.

"Sit down."

"We want to eat."

"Is this how they waste your time in that school? No wonder you're so stupid."

His uncle tossed a roll, which hit Sal in the side of the head, and the whole table started to laugh. Sal sat down, looked into his plate, and a few tears ran down his cheek. Someone shouted, "Now he's crying!" "Poems and tears. What kind of sissy are you raising anyway?"

"Goddamn sons of bitches," Sal thought. He wanted to kill them all. "I hope they all choke on their food." He felt like taking his fork and shoving it into his uncle's fat face. From that moment, any creativity that Sal had was stifled, especially in front of his family. When he did a good job on an art assignment, he begged his teachers not to tell his parents. He refused to take music lessons; he never again tried to write poetry; and he began to ridicule others whenever they exhibited any sensitivity.

Is Your Son Angry?

Maybe you were an angry boy and didn't even know it. (Maybe you didn't even know you were an angry man until 20 pages ago!) Maybe now you are worried that your own son is going to follow you down the sorrowful road of chronic anger. Maybe you would like to be a positive influence in the life of an angry boy. In order to make a difference, you have to know what you are dealing with.

What does excess anger look like in a child? This is not easy to pin down; there aren't many hard and fast symptoms. But very often it looks just like anger in an adult—if you have an explosive temper now, you probably also flew into rages as a child.

The fine line that keeps men in control when they're angry (sometimes, at least) is much, much finer in boys. Volatile angry men can often feel their anger building for some time before they explode—they have been through it so many times that can usually recognize the danger signs. (That doesn't mean that they do anything about it!) A boy doesn't have that experience or sense of perspective. A boy comes to his boiling point more rapidly. His emotions—whether positive or negative—are very close to the surface. The spontaneity that we often admire in children's emotions is enchanting and refreshing when they are happy but is a problem when it comes to anger. A boy is not as likely to realize that he is getting angry, and he doesn't have the maturity to control himself.

Children are much more vulnerable than adults to the effects of what happens to them, for good or ill. You can probably remember things that happened to you as a child that made you extremely embarrassed, unhappy, or furious. Now that you're an adult, you realize that the things that seemed so important at the time were nothing to get so upset about. You look back and wonder why it all seemed like such a big deal. But of course: you've matured! You have learned better ways of protecting yourself. You have had many more experiences and you have gained perspective. The first time a girl broke up with you, it felt like your world was going to end. The tenth time it happened, it probably was not as devastating.

Angry boys are caught in a troublesome dilemma. On the one hand, they have more difficulty controlling themselves when they get angry. But on the other hand, it's almost as though more control is expected of them than of adults. To them, it seems that every adult on the planet is telling them how to act, what to do, and when to do it. If you, as an adult, scream and curse, you may get disapproving looks from people and may eventually suffer weightier consequences, like losing your job. But if your son does that, all the adults in his life immediately come down on him like a ton of bricks. Even though boys are in training and adults are supposed to tell them what to do (and even punish them for good reason), it doesn't make it any easier for them to handle their feelings. All it comes down to for them is that they have to conform their

185

behavior to the expectations of parents, teachers, and other adults. This leads many boys to stuff down their anger; they seethe on the inside and can only express their turmoil indirectly.

Portrait of an Angry Boy

This indirect expression of anger can be seen in the pictures boys draw. Psychologists have long used children's drawings as an integral part of a psychological evaluation. Violent drawings are often about anger; drawings of people being hurt can be an outlet for frustration and desire for retaliation against offenders. It is not safe for young boys to aggress directly against their "enemies," who are bigger and more powerful than they are, so drawing is a way to express their anger.

The drawings of angry boys often depict people with larger-than-life teeth. When drawing families, boys will portray many of the conflicts that they are experiencing with parents or other individuals. They sometimes draw themselves exploding like a bomb, shooting at family members, or otherwise expressing their anger.

Are all graphic drawings necessarily signs of anger problems? After all, many boys have a fascination with mechanized mayhem; they like to draw pictures of military machines, guns, bullets, and explosions. I can only tell you that most well-adjusted boys do not routinely draw scenes of extreme violence or violence toward family. Also, drawings of *interpersonal* violence are problematic. If you find drawings of knifings, graphic injuries, and especially malevolent faces, your son could have a problem with anger.

You can also spot an angry boy by the way he treats his siblings and pets. While most children argue and occasionally fight with each other, there is a point when the fighting is too much. If your son gets into too many fights, if he gets excessively violent when he loses his temper, he has a problem with anger. If he is leaving bruises on his brothers and sisters, he has a problem. If his temper results in cuts, broken bones, or other significant injuries, there is little doubt that you've got a problem on your hands. This is especially true if the ones getting hurt are much younger and smaller than he is. Most boys are animal lovers, so if your son is hurting animals, take note. Something is not right. He has too much anger and he does not know how to handle these intense feelings.

Another form that anger can take, especially in older boys, is excessive rebelliousness and opposition to authority. Angry boys will often refuse to cooperate, even in small matters, for no apparent reason. A good reason for almost any behavior is that it makes the adults in his life mad at him. Hairstyle is often a good focus for this expression. It doesn't matter how goofy the cut looks to an adult. If adults don't like it, the angry boy will wear it. The same goes for clothing.

Of course, some rebelliousness is part of being a certain age. Boys need to stretch and find the limits. It's going to be a judgment call, but too much rebellion is a warning sign. For example, many schools in the South have banned T-shirts that depict the Confederate battle flag from their campuses; to African Americans, this flag is considered a symbol of injustice and oppression. If a boy wears one to school anyway, it's a pretty good bet that he has a problem with anger. If a boy repeatedly refuses direct orders from school officials, cops, or other authority figures, he has a problem with anger.

Vandalism and practical jokes can also be ways that boys express their anger. And again, it is difficult to be black and white about what is a normal kid prank and what goes over the line. Soaping someone's windows on Halloween is not as bad as slashing tires. And *any* setting of fires is abnormal. One of the hallmarks of young arsonists (who are almost always male) is intense rage that they are not able to deal with or express directly. So they commit the ultimate in passive aggression: burning things. Many boys go through a practical joke stage; this is not abnormal. However, if your son is constantly playing practical jokes on other people, or if his jokes are cruel or cause injury, this is not normal.

If a boy not only engages in forbidden behavior, such as smoking in school, but does it blatantly and knowing that he will get caught, he has a problem with anger. Again, some level of defiance is occasionally evident in most boys. But a boy who repeatedly "gets in the face" of adults has a problem with anger.

Many boys show their anger for the first time when they get involved in competitive sports. Part of the psychological growth that is supposed to take place when a boy begins to compete is learning to lose. This was particularly hard for me when I was a boy. I can remember coming home from my first competitive basketball game when I was 9 or 10 years old. We had lost the game and I was in a foul mood—I didn't even know why I was so grumpy. But my mother picked up on it right away and told me that if I didn't learn to take losing in stride, I would not be allowed to play anymore. Difficulty accepting defeat is also seen in excessive aggression and fighting during sports. A football player can hit hard, but there is a difference between hitting hard and hitting to hurt. Taunting opponents, fighting, and on-field disrespect for opposing players, referees, and coaches can be a sign of poorly controlled anger.

 Angry boys also often train harder than others do. They will practice longer than other boys and don't seem to have the perspective that there are other important things in life. Although this single-minded dedication is probably necessary to reach college or Olympic levels of skill, let's face it: most boys are not going to compete in college or the Olympics. They need to develop the perspective that girls, fishing, academics, chess, or a hundred other pursuits are also important.

Teenage Meltdown

It can be especially difficult to separate excess anger from "normal" growing pains when boys begin to enter adolescence. The changes taking place in their bodies are a sign that changes are also taking place in their heads. These changes do not happen harmoniously and in synch.

A boy's voice may change long before he starts to grow body hair or develop adult muscles. Similarly, a boy's desire to be independent may develop sooner than his ability to do so. His sexual fires may become lit sooner than his ability to conduct himself responsibly. Adult feelings pop out before the ability to handle those feelings is in place. The experiences of love, rejection, jealousy, humiliation, and anger are all more intense in adolescence, partly because the necessary coping skills and behavioral controls are not yet in place. It's like someone put the fuel rods into the nuclear reactor before they installed the control rods. If the psychological control rods don't develop, the boy is headed for a meltdown.

What happens when a boy hits meltdown stage? He assaults someone in anger. He commits suicide during a depressive episode. He gets injured during a joy ride in a stolen car. He ruins his future by getting convicted of an impulsive crime. Most violent crime is committed by young men. According to FBI statistics, men 15 to 30 years of age account for 46 percent of arrests for violent crimes. However, according to U.S. Census Bureau statistics, males in this age bracket make up only 21 percent of the population. One fifth of the U.S. population accounts for almost half of the violent crime.

In my role as a forensic psychologist, I spend a lot of time with people awaiting trial for serious offenses. Most of these people are male and most of them are between the ages of 16 and 25—boys who have hit serious meltdown. It is heartbreaking to review their records and see the picture of the cute, smiling 10-year-old and then the mug shot of the snarling 17-year-old arrested for a brutal murder. What happened in between?

For a lot of these boys, the story is the same. Most have no adult males in their lives. Most do not even know who their fathers are. Many have lived hand-to-mouth, never knowing if there would be food on the table, heat in the house, or lights to do homework by. Many have had to assume the role of parent for younger brothers and sisters because their own parents were absent for long periods of time, were drug abusers or prostitutes, or were children themselves. Most have never had a stable home for more than several months at a time; they have lived with grandparents, friends, or on the streets. Most have never been exposed to guiding and constructive discipline; rather, they experienced beatings or other punishment when some adult was in a bad mood. When they got to school and teachers tried to instill some discipline, they rebelled and eventually left school in the 10th or 11th grade. Many have seen more shootings and assaults than they have paychecks.

"Wolf" was 17 when I met him in the county jail. He was awaiting trial for first-degree murder in the drive-by shooting of another young man in the neighborhood next to his. He told me that he was in the back seat of a car being driven by one of his friends. He had been drinking enough booze and smoking enough weed that he had almost passed out. As they rode by a darkened house, one of the other boys shouted "Wet him, Wolf! Wet him!" ("Wet" is slang for "shoot.") Wolf said he pointed a large-caliber handgun in the direction of the porch and began to pull the trigger, never seeing anyone or knowing if anyone was really there.

Wolf grew up in a rough neighborhood. The several blocks of his neighborhood, Laura Sands, is known to police as a dangerous area, populated by organized gangs, narcotics dealers, and prostitutes. Gunshots are heard every night and crime is endemic. Wolf got his nickname from an uncle who liked the image of a predator. Wolf never knew his father, and his mother was not even sure who his father was. She was a crack addict who supported her habit by trading sex for "rocks." She was frequently out all night and virtually incoherent when she did get home. She often came home injured from fights with pimps, customers, or other hookers. Half the time, her customers came home with her. Wolf watched her have sex from as far back as he could remember.

Wolf had to start fending for himself before he was even in school. He told me that he would go to his grandmother's house or to the neighbors' when he ran out of food. The house was filthy. The power and water were often cut off for non-payment, and Wolf never had a quiet place to do his homework. He started spending time roaming the neighborhood and hanging out with older boys who gave him food and companionship. But the little world of Laura Sands was violent. We sat in the jail and counted the number of serious assaults that he had witnessed in his 17 years. Just limiting the count to gunshot wounds, Wolf had seen more than 25 assaults before he even graduated from high school. He knew a lot about human anatomy from seeing it on display after shootings.

Wolf and his friends used to play a game in which they drove into a rival neighborhood looking for other young men hanging out on the streets. They would then race by, shooting their guns in the general direction of the rivals, and shout "Coulda had you!" They also played "tag," but a version quite different from the traditional children's game. This version involved driving into an unfriendly neighborhood and trying to run over rival gang members. They scored points based on the importance of the gang member and the severity of the injuries.

As with many boys who grow up unsupervised, Wolf didn't trust anyone. He had many girlfriends ("bitches"), but had no intention of getting serious with them, because "women will use you." He frequently lied to me and to his attorney, even though he knew that we might have been the only forces standing between him and the death penalty. Wolf had no remorse for the man who died as a result of his drunken, blind shooting. He told me that it was "him or me" and believed that he would also be shot someday, that it was inevitable. He had been shot at many times, but never hit. He had vivid descriptions of the different sounds that different caliber bullets make as they sing by in the air or ricochet off different objects.

Wolf has never had a birthday party; he has never had a parent go to a PTA meeting; he learned about sex on the streets; he has never been to the dentist; and he is deeply, profoundly, and pathologically angry. Wolf accepted a plea-bargain and pleaded guilty to second-degree murder. He is now in prison. Wolf will be middle-aged before he next goes to a ball game, talks to a pretty girl, has a beer, or evens chooses his own clothing.

Of course, not all angry boys experience the extremes of deprivation, neglect, and violence that Wolf has. But a large number of angry boys have not been tended as they should. Maybe Dad worked long hours and was too tired to mess around or help with homework when he got home. Maybe Mom was exhausted too and wasn't so nurturing and attentive after her own eight-hour workday. Maybe these boys were punished more out of their parents' frustrations than for their actual behavior. Maybe their parents or their teachers used humiliation and guilt as disciplinary tools. Maybe they were disrespected in other ways.

How to Create an Angry Boy

It's not hard to create an angry boy. Just about any adult can do it. Anger in boys comes from the same place it comes from in men. All it takes is disrespect. Anger in boys comes from physical abuse. It comes from humiliation. It comes from frustration. It comes from shame. It comes from anything that teaches the boy that he is worthless. Not sure if you are efficiently making your son angry? Just follow these easy step-by-step instructions.

Make sure you frequently humiliate him

Shaming as a disciplinary technique teaches the boy that the world thinks he is inferior. As a boy, I attended a Catholic school and was taught by nuns who were big on confrontation and humiliation. Their idea of discipline for a minor infraction (such as talking while waiting in line) was to hang a sign around the criminal's neck that read "I am a baby" and parade him through the classrooms of the lower grades. I underwent this punishment twice and suffered the embarrassment of being marched through my younger brother's class. I can assure you that, whatever other effects this punishment had on me, it made me furious and contributed to my lasting distrust of authority.

Parents and other adults who use shame as a major disciplinary tool are sending boys down the road to being permanently ashamed of themselves. When a boy experiences shame and humiliation on a frequent basis, anything associated with that shame will begin to elicit the shame regardless of whether the boy has done anything wrong. For example, if a boy was excessively shamed with regard to masturbation or other sexual activity, he will feel shame whenever he is sexually aroused or active. If he was shamed when he made mistakes, he will probably become timid, be unwilling to take chances, and avoid adventure. Not only that, but those who induced the shame also become associated with it. That's right, you! He will be ashamed and nervous around you.

Ignore him

Most boys crave attention. They love it when their parents, especially their fathers, see their good homework, come to their games, and take them fishing. If you let your son grow up without you in the picture, he will be angry with you and wonder why you don't love him. He will see the other boys with their fathers and he will come to believe that you don't care about him.

Even though you never physically abuse your son or do anything in particular to damage him emotionally, your job as a parent does not stop there. It is not enough to refrain from treating badly. You must be an active force in his life. It is easy to get so wrapped up in your work, the rest of your family, or whatever interests you in life that you forget to pay attention to your son. Boys need adult guidance, comfort, reassurance, and discipline. They need to know that you care about them.

In Sal's case, he was never physically or sexually abused. Humiliation like the scene at dinner was not a daily occurrence. But the adults in his life never invested much time or interest in him. The only interest they took in his education was to scream at him if he got bad grades. They never went to PTA meetings, talked to his teachers, taught him how to play basketball, or even asked where he was going when he left the house. Children were to be seen and not heard, and when Sal did try to talk to his mother or father, they either answered briefly or told him to be quiet because they were watching television. Sal tried hanging out with a friend whose father played with them both, but it wasn't a substitute for attention from the adults in his own life. As Sal got older, he began to wonder if there was something wrong with him or if his parents were really his biological parents because he could come up with no other explanations for how they treated him. The neglect felt like continual rejection, which fed his anger.

Show him you disrespect him by harming him physically

Hitting a child is a sure-fire way to show him he is worthless and that you don't care about him. It is supremely disrespectful. Hitting in the head and face is an insult. Is it any wonder that men used to challenge each other to a duel by slapping the face? Is it a coincidence that people respond to an insult by throwing drinks into the face of the insulter? When you hit a child in the face, you are telling him that he has no dignity or right to respect. This causes anger. Indeed, this causes rage.

More serious physical abuse and sexual abuse are extreme cases of how adults can disrespect children. The victims of such abuse may never recover from the emotional and psychological damage caused by this very basic violation of their dignity. Abuse teaches boys that they are inferior. They come to think of themselves as fundamentally bad. The abuse causes them to be profoundly embarrassed about what they have endured and about themselves as people. The abuse tells them that they are objects, that they have no rights or dignity, and that they exist only to be used for someone else's purposes.

Physical and sexual abuse also distort a boy's ideas of how to interact with other people. They teach him that the way to get what you want in life is to take it. It teaches him that other people are there to be used. Sexually abused boys have great difficulty ever having a normal sex life. Sex will always be a source of anxiety to them. Is it at all surprising that most perpetrators of physical and sexual child abuse were themselves abused as children? If you learn, when you are young and weak, that weak people are merely objects to be used by the strong, what do you do when you have become strong and you want something from someone weaker than you? You aggress, use, and abuse them because that is what you know how to do.

Several years ago, I evaluated an inmate who was convicted of a murder that he committed when he was 17 years old. He had killed a prostitute when she snatched some crack out of his hand and ran. She was sick and debilitated, and her attempt to get away with the drugs made him laugh. He was a big boy and easily ran her down and caught her. He then beat her head against some railroad tracks until she was unrecognizable and walked two blocks to his house.

As I got into his school and health records, I found the most appalling record of physical abuse by his father. I encountered entry after entry about bruises, broken bones, attempts to run away, and finally, when he was 11 or 12, assaults against his father.

This young man wasn't even able to tell me why he killed the woman. "Did you get the drugs back?" I asked. "Yeah." "Did she hit you or try to hurt you?" "No." "Why did you keep hitting her?" "I was mad." Period. This boy had already made more than $1,000 that night from his drug sales and the prostitute stole less than $25 worth. "I was mad." *I was mad.*

How to Save Your Angry Boy

Have you identified your son or nephew in the descriptions above? Do you recognize someone who fits the pattern on the football team that you coach? Maybe you can make a difference. It is never too late to make a difference in a boy's life. There *are* helpful things that you can do. But the first thing that you have to do is decide that you want to help. This involves commitment over the long haul. You can't take a kid fishing once or twice and decide that you have done your part. You have to make a substantial investment of your time and attention. What is maybe even worse than neglect of your boy is a half-assed effort. When you build a kid's hopes up and then let him down, you scrape the scabs off of the wounds that are trying to heal and he has to start all over again getting over the latest disappointment. This is particularly true in the case of divorced parents. If you say that you are going to pick your son up for the day, *do it.* If you make him a promise, *keep it.* He is counting on you. I can't begin to enumerate the times that I have listened to a patient describe a childhood spent sitting by the window, waiting for Dad to come, hours after the time he said he would be there.

Go easy on the shame
Remember that it is not necessary to shame a child for every little thing that he does wrong. Shame is an appropriate device for disciplining a boy, in moderation. We are supposed to feel ashamed when we do something that is unacceptable. But don't overdo it. Save it for the significant screw-ups. A little shame goes a long way.

Teach him the difference between bad behavior and a bad person

It is especially important to remember to aim your criticism at the child's behavior, not the child as a person. Bad behavior can be changed. Bad boys presumably cannot. And boys who are taught to believe that they are bad boys grow up believing that they are fundamentally inferior to others. Like shame and humiliation, a belief in one's inferiority leads to anger.

Focus on the positive

We know from years of psychological research that rewarding good behavior is much more effective than punishing bad behavior. Notice that I am not focusing on what a boy deserves, but on what is more effective. Positive reinforcement is much more effective than punishment in producing behavior change. I can hear you now: "I shouldn't have to pay him to do the things he should do." I argue with parents of uncontrolled boys about this all the time. And I always ask them, "What is more important, for you to be right about what your son should do or for him to get his chores done?"

Whatever your beliefs regarding what *should* happen to boys who screw up, make no mistake, it works better to praise and reward him for doing what you want him to do than it does to scream at him, hit him, or ground him for doing what you don't want him to do. For example, you will get more As out of your student by rewarding him with more privileges (some parents even pay for As) than by grounding him a week for each C. Think about your own workplace. Would you be more motivated and satisfied if your company gave you bonuses or perks for good work or reprimanded you and docked your pay for mediocre work?

It may seem to you that I am saying that punishment produces angry boys and that boys should not be punished. I am not saying that boys should never be punished. Punishment has its role in disciplining a child. But all too often, parents punish out of their own anger or frustration rather than as a teaching tool. "Spare the rod and spoil the child" has been misinterpreted, in my opinion. The rod mentioned in this saying should be thought of as a shepherd's staff. This rod is used to guide the sheep, not to hit them. Physical punishment should be used sparingly, if at all. Striking a child should be restricted to putting an immediate stop to dangerous behavior, such as setting fires or running out into the street. And children should never be hit in the head: not only is it disrespectful, it is dangerous and can easily produce injury.

Be patient

Rome wasn't built in a day. Your boy has had years to get the way he is now. You are not going to make significant changes in a week or two. You may expect him to be all over you with gratitude for every little thing that you do for him. But he has probably grown wary. He is not used to the changes that you have decided to make. And remember, everyone is suspicious of change. It will take some time for him to get used to the new rules. He will disappoint you from time to time. It may seem like he is doing well for days or weeks and then he may lose his temper for no good reason. He is learning, and no one learns anything in one fell swoop.

Recognize your limitations

Forget the notion that you can "fix" your boy's anger completely. You can't. For one thing, you do not have complete control over him. Your influence is limited, and the older he gets the less influence you will have. Other children, teachers, coaches, and society exercise powerful influences over the boy that he is and the man that he will become.

Not only is your influence increasingly limited, but he is responsible for his own behavior, more so the older he gets. This is where trust comes into play. You have no choice but to try to trust him, because he will be out of your sight and acting on his own much of the day. But to demonstrate that you do trust him goes a long way toward building his self-confidence and pride in himself.

As with many of the issues that I have discussed, dealing with your angry son may be more than you can handle. He may have gotten so far out of your reach that you can do little for him. Maybe the streets have swallowed him up. Maybe you and he are so alienated that you have no more influence over him. Maybe you just don't know how to deal with kids. If so, get some professional help. Try to get your son to the attention of his guidance counselor, favorite teacher, or school psychologist. If this doesn't seem to be enough, get him to a mental health center or to a private psychiatrist or psychologist.

Epilogue: Angry Boys and School Shootings

As I was putting the final touches on this chapter, all hell seemed to break loose in many of our schools. Children are getting guns and shooting their classmates and teachers for trivial reasons. At least the reasons seem to be trivial on the surface: "The jocks made fun of me" or "We don't fit in." What has happened to warp these children's perspectives so severely that they think that the solution to their feelings of alienation is to grab a gun and kill anyone they see?

Rest assured that the responsibility lies very little with the children. They do not yet have the psychological sophistication to be held accountable in the same way that adults are. Something in our home environments or national atmospheres is creating the anger and the awful despair and suggesting this drastic remedy. And the violence is no longer concentrated in poor, inner-city neighborhoods. We seem to be reaping the fruits of anger that we have sown without respect to income, race, or geographical location, and reaping in a deadly way.

19

FOR THE WOMEN
how to help yourself and your men

You, the mothers, wives, girlfriends, and sisters of angry men, have had to carry almost as heavy a burden as your men. This chapter is an attempt to address your needs, wants, desires, and responsibilities as you try to live with an angry man. I will also try to provide you with some specific suggestions for how to handle his anger and how to help end the cycle of anger in your relationship—even if that means leaving your angry man altogether.

It's Not Your Fault

Probably the first thing that every woman in a relationship with an angry man should realize is that his anger is not her fault. Many angry men are reluctant to admit any of their flaws and shortcomings, so they will try to find others to blame for their problems. And you will be the one he blames, because you have the most intense relationship with him. You know him better than anyone else, and he knows that you can see through most of his bullshit. You know when he is lying to someone about how much money he makes. You were there when he failed to get his promotion. You know that he sometimes has problems with his erection. You may therefore be a threat to him, and he will feel less threatened if he can somehow shift the responsibility for his actions to you. So you will become the reason for everything that goes wrong in his life.

You are the one who he abuses, verbally or physically, and this makes him feel guilty. It may seem weird, but at the same time that he feels guilty for the things that he says and does to you, the fact that he feels guilty makes him more angry. And since you are the one that he feels guilty about, you are the one that is the focus of this part of his anger. You are probably only the latest of several girls and women in his life who have had this dubious honor, beginning with Mom, of course!

There is a long tradition, at least in European and American history, of blaming the mother for the son's problems. Sigmund Freud had a big hand in this, although he was certainly echoing a tradition that preceded him. For Freud, all of a person's problems were the result of childhood experiences interacting with a pre-programmed series of stages that a child goes through as he ages. If mother weans her son too soon, it causes problems. If toilet training is harsh, it causes problems. If mother does any little thing wrong, her son will be ruined for life and it's all her fault. Notice that while Freud concentrated almost exclusively on the development of boys and men, his focus on the role of parenting was almost exclusively on the effects of mothers. So, men are the hapless victims of inept, evil, or "neurotic" mothers.

Even after people began to question and discard much of what Freud had to say, the tradition of blaming the mother for the problems of their sons continued, even in the supposedly enlightened arena of psychological and medical research. In the 1960s and 1970s, "cold and distant" mothers were blamed for causing schizophrenia in their children. (We are now fairly certain that schizophrenia is in fact a genetic disorder that has little to do with how a child is raised. And the supposedly cold and distant mothers were probably made that way by the incredibly difficult task of raising a seriously disordered child without much help from Dad.) Even today, the debate rages on in psychology and society in general over whether mothers who work (and place their children with caretakers during the day) are to blame for all of the problems caused by young men.

Mothers, you are not to blame for the things that your sons do in their anger. They are responsible for their own behavior. That is not to say that the way a boy is raised has nothing to do with his anger. That may sound contradictory, but let me explain. Of course, if you abuse your son, it will be a big factor in his anger. You should not abuse your son. It doesn't take a genius to figure that one out. But maybe you were doing the best you could.

In sorting out what you are responsible for, we have to ask why you abused your son. Did you do so because he was a difficult child and you were an unskilled parent? Are you an angry woman? Why were you angry? Were you abusing drugs or alcohol? Was it self-medication to try to deal with your own misery? Were you being abused yourself while you were trying to be a mother? Were you abused by your parents? Were you abused by the men in your life? Were you abandoned by your son's father? None of these factors are *excuses* for being a poor parent. But they are reasons why you might have done a less-than-perfect job.

Notice that the focus of these questions is to explain rather than blame. These questions focus on your behavior rather than upon your goodness or badness as a person. Very few mothers are deliberately harmful to their sons. Very few mothers are evil in this way—and make no mistake, to deliberately harm a child is evil. Mothers do what they do for other reasons, and most women try to do their best. But we all make mistakes. I assure you that you could have been a better mother. *All* mothers could have been better mothers. Just as your son has to move beyond blaming you and focus on improving his life, you accomplish nothing by continuing to blame yourself. You must also move on, even if your son does not.

Besides, once he became a man, your son became responsible for his own behavior. None of us was raised in a perfect world. We all have personal baggage. Most of us have been hurt, lied to, and taken advantage of at one time or another. We are each responsible for picking up the pieces and moving ahead. We each have to take our lives into our own two hands and make them the best that we can. Your son, or boyfriend, or husband is avoiding his responsibility as a man if he continues to blame you for his feelings and behavior. Being a good man takes work, and it is work that you cannot do for the man in your life. It is up to him to make his life the way he wants it to be.

Move beyond Blame

In my role as a psychologist, I encourage angry men to look back to see where they became angry. I sometimes have them write autobiographies, or make audiotapes, or just sit and think about all their past pain and hurt. I ask them to be honest with themselves about how they felt when their parents mistreated them in both big and small ways: when the neighborhood bully beat them up, when the teacher humiliated them, or when Dad treated another brother or sister better. This is an important part of the coping process. So many angry men have walled themselves off from their feelings and from their unpleasant memories that they truly do not know why they are angry.

In the early stages of therapy, it is important for them to recognize and acknowledge the times that they have been mistreated. Remember that deep inside, many men feel unworthy of happiness and deserving of punishment. It is often a great relief to them to realize that they did not deserve some of the treatment that they received.

Then, as the angry man proceeds in his therapy, I encourage him to move beyond blaming. To put too much emphasis on blame is to put the emphasis in the wrong place.

One of the first things to do at this stage is to discuss what his role was in these hurtful incidents. What did he do to make things worse? What could he have done to lessen the impact of the situations that hurt him? Again, this is not blaming. It represents two things that I want the angry man to realize. First, he must begin to get the feeling of control over what happens to him. Your man needs to feel as though his efforts can potentially be rewarded; he needs to feel as though there is a reason to try. By focusing on his role in his own pain, even though it is temporarily uncomfortable for him, he may begin to develop more confidence in his ability to shape his own destiny. Then he can realize the second important thing—how to focus his attention on his and others' *behavior,* rather than on their goodness or badness as persons.

This distinction is extremely important and is one that I hope angry men and the women in their lives take away from reading this book. This theme reflects my belief that people in pain should focus on their behavior, rather than applying labels to themselves or other people. Behavior can be changed; people cannot. By that, I mean that if you believe that you are fundamentally screwed up, or worthless, or damned, what can you do to change your lot? Nothing. The saying goes that you cannot make a silk purse out of a sow's ear. In this context, that proverb encourages hopelessness. As a therapist, it infuriates me (privately, of course!) when patients tell me that they are "too old" to change their behavior or that "you can't teach an old dog new tricks." People *can* change their behavior, at any stage of life. Coming to believe this is an important part of your man's attempts to put his anger in its rightful place.

You Can't Fix Him

In general, American culture teaches women that they are supposed to nurture, comfort, heal, feed, protect, and make sacrifices for, well, everyone. A woman's own needs are supposed to come second, or third, after everyone else has been taken care of. The trouble with this ethic is that many women's needs never get seen to. By the time everyone else is taken care of, it's time to go to bed and start all over again the next day.

In particular, women are taught (directly or indirectly) that it is their job to be subordinate to men and to put the men's needs and wants before their own. A woman is supposed to "stand by her man." Many women come to believe that it is their job to "fix" everyone that they come into contact with. These women define their role in life very narrowly. They come to see themselves as having little other purpose in life other than providing for the comfort and happiness of others. Suddenly, everyone else's problems become the woman's problems.

With regard to the angry man in her life, the woman is programmed to believe that she must be doing something wrong in order for him to act the way that he does. If he is angry and abusive when he comes home from work, it must be because she doesn't have dinner ready on time, or she is not keeping the kids quiet enough, or she says annoying things. If he is not satisfied with their sex life, it must be her fault. It couldn't possibly be because his demands are unreasonable.

Let's examine the ways you may consider yourself the "fixer" in your relationship. If your man had an affair, did you feel as though you must not be a good sex partner? Did you consider buying sexy underwear and videotapes to learn more sexual techniques? If you and your husband decided that your child needed more parental supervision, which of you quit your job to stay home? When a conflict arises between his job and yours, who makes the sacrifices? Who takes the sick kids to the doctor? Who serves as the mediator between feuding family members? Probably you, the woman.

The woman who falls into the "fixer" role begins to constrict her life more and more to try to please her man. She stops seeing any friends that he doesn't like (which is usually just about all of them, especially if they're men). She sees her family less and less because they get on his nerves. She doesn't dance anymore because he accuses her of trying to attract other men. She doesn't go out with her girlfriends anymore because he wants her to spend his free time with him. Even the food they eat is what he wants to eat. The woman is gradually but increasingly "deselfed." She gives up more and more of herself in order to make things better between them. Somewhere along the way, she has totally lost track of who she once was. She no longer knows what she likes, what she did for fun, even what her opinions are.

And all this sacrificing doesn't work! The more you sacrifice and try to please him, the more he continues along his angry way. Your efforts are to no avail. *You have got to back off!* You cannot change these things about him. You cannot fix his problems. It is futile for you to continue to try to mold yourself into what you think he wants you to be in a vain attempt to make him happy.

Why are your attempts to fix your angry man's problems destined to fail? First and foremost, because you are not the source of his unhappiness. The things that you are trying to change are not the things that are really causing his anger. You cannot change the important things that are the sources of his anger—things that are inside of him and that only he can change . It is up to him to deal with his poor tolerance for frustration. It is his job to stop letting little things get blown out of proportion. Only he can decide to become more assertive and get his own needs met. You cannot do these things for another person.

You must learn to differentiate between his business and yours. You must learn to define more clearly the boundaries between what you are responsible for and what you are not responsible for. You must learn to let other people take care of themselves. For example, it is not your job to buy his family's Christmas presents so that their feelings will not be hurt. It is not your job to send his mother a Mother's Day card. It is not your job to give up all of your friends because he doesn't like them. It is not your job to completely suppress your opinions and adopt his. Not only is it not your job, *but it won't work.* Women who do suppress all of themselves in order to appease their men end up frustrated and tired . . . and he is still angry.

It is not hard for most women to acknowledge that trying to fix an angry man is futile. But you may never have thought about the possibility that your attempts to help him in this way may actually be making things worse, both for you and for him. Being a fixer makes things worse for you because you will feel like a failure when nothing you try to do for your man makes any difference in him or your relationship. This contributes to depression in many women. Two of the most important symptoms of depression are feelings of hopelessness and feelings of helplessness.

Trying to fix your man actually may make him worse. Why? For one thing, it gives him an excuse for his bad behavior. If you are continually scurrying around trying to make everything right, he can blame you when his behavior gets out of line or when he continues to be angry. It allows him to put the responsibility for his life onto you instead of taking responsibility for his own destiny. In addition, if you are making all the effort, he never learns how to take care of himself. If you are continually running interference between him and the world, his own social skills atrophy. How many times have you gone to the PTA meeting because your husband says that he "doesn't know what to do"? When you are the one who keeps up contact with his family, he loses the ability to deal with them himself. When you hush the children or hurry them out of sight, what do you think happens to his ability to be a father? When you try to smooth over every bump in his life and head off every possible frustration, he loses the ability to do it himself. "Use it or lose it" is true for many areas of life, including our ability to deal with our emotions and our social lives.

What *Can* You Do for Him?

So far, we've learned many of the things that you cannot do or should not try to do for your angry man. What can you do to help him out? This is going to be difficult to specify. In *The Dance of Anger,* Harriet Lerner refers to "over-functioning" and "under-functioning" in relationships. Over-functioning is when you are doing someone else's work; under-functioning is when you depend on others to do things for you that you should do for yourself. Sometimes it is difficult to determine the difference between helping and over-functioning. You will have to learn to look at your behavior, your angry man's behavior, and your relationship in some fundamentally different ways and make some difficult decisions that he will not like.

It will be difficult to make even minor changes in the way that you interact with your angry man. You have developed some pretty strong habits, and any habits are hard to break. But the habits that you have developed have been strengthened by the intense emotional climate that has surrounded your relationship. When you get scared, or depressed, or nervous, you will have a tendency to go back to your old ways of behaving. For many people, an unhappy but predictable pattern is preferable to the unknown. This is most tragically illustrated by a tendency among abused women to provoke their husbands until the husbands explode and hit them. Many of these women will tell you that whenever their man gets angry, he tends to hit them. They can't stand the waiting and the horrible verbal abuse that comes before the hitting. So these women will push him and deliberately make him madder until he hits them in order to "get it over with."

You will also have difficulty changing your behavior because your angry man will resist any attempt you make to change. He is comfortable (but probably not happy) with your relationship as well. He will put pressure on you to continue in the role that you have been in. He will resist any show of independence on your part. He will make a scene if you want to spend time with your friends. He will blame you for his unhappiness. And he will use all of the verbally, emotionally, and maybe physically abusive strategies that he has always used to keep you in line.

Angry men do not have much self-confidence. Very often, they do not think very highly of themselves. You can help him develop his self-confidence by letting him know when he does things that you admire. But be honest; don't make things up. We all like to feel that others admire us. If you do admire him, let him know. If he has a difficult interview coming up or some other type of challenge, express your confidence in him. Let him know that you think he will do well. But do not be hypocritical—if you cannot say something honestly, it is better to say nothing at all.

Remember that you will get nowhere trying to win arguments with him. Most of the arguments that you have been having are probably not that important anyway. One of the first things you learn in any kind of training for negotiation is to find a way to let the other person get out of a difficult situation while saving face. If you want to get somewhere with an angry man, it is best not to try to shame or humiliate him. He will just dig his heels in and get more stubborn. Forcing someone to give in or admit that they are wrong is not a productive way to deal with conflict. Instead, try to arrange things so that you both come out on top. For example, many arguments start out over trivia, like "Which movie are we going to see?" Soon, the argument becomes a contest that neither person wants to lose. "We always see the movies that you want to see." Before the argument intensifies to an ego-threatening level, find a compromise. "How about if we see your movie tonight and come back tomorrow and see the one that I want to see?" Or the two of you could each see your own movie, meet back in the lobby, and go out for coffee afterwards and tell each other about the movies.

It may seem like the list of things that you can do for him is short. It is. It may seem like a version of "tough love." It is. When you get right down to it, there is not a whole lot that you can do for another person. Your angry man has some holes in his personality. You are doing him no favors by trying to fill those holes for him. Back off!

What Can You Do for Yourself?

Your angry man may be pulling you both down. It is important that you not let him destroy you or your life. This may mean that you have to leave him in order to save yourself. But this is better than both of you being destroyed. Let's talk about how to decide whether to stay or go right off the bat.

If you have been physically abused by your man, chances are that it will happen again. Past violence predicts future violence, and the violence usually gets worse. According to the American Bar Association, "domestic violence is an ongoing cycle producing increasingly severe injuries over time." According to statistics compiled by the ABA, 32 percent of battered women are victimized again within six months. Forty-seven percent of men who beat their wives do so at least three times per year.

Always remember, *there is no excuse for hitting another person, especially for a man to hit a woman.* There is nothing that you can do to justify getting hit, unless you yourself are so violent that your man has had to fight back in self-defense. This is rare. There is nothing you can say; there is nothing that you can do; there is no failure on your part that is a good reason for him to hit you. If he has hit you, you must reach down deep inside and find the self-respect that you have lost. You must conclude that your self-respect demands that others treat you with respect as well. At the very least, you must tell him that if he ever hits you again, you will prosecute him. *And then you must follow through.* Don't ever make empty threats. If you say you will do something, do it! But you must decide that you will not allow yourself to be used by him and treated with this ultimate form of disrespect.

If you have been physically abused, there is a good chance that you should leave the relationship. For your own safety, do not ever deliberately antagonize your angry man. Do not try to make him hit you to "get it over with." If you are afraid that a situation is getting out of hand, leave immediately. I often advise the wives of abusive husbands to keep a bag packed with a week's worth of clothes, $250, an extra set of house and car keys, toiletries, and anything else that you will need if you have to leave quickly and stay away for a week.

You should also consider leaving the relationship if your man stubbornly refuses to take any responsibility for the difficulties between the two of you. You *know* that you are not the one causing all of the problems. If he refuses to acknowledge his role, he will never change. Be honest with yourself about what your life has been like. Don't deny or minimize the problems that exist. If you believe that he will never change, you must leave him.

This is not an easy decision to make, and practical considerations come into play as well. The first such consideration is the children. Many couples stay together "for the kids," even when both of them would rather be divorced. Make no mistake: It is not healthy for children to be raised in an environment of physical abuse or continual strife. For one thing, it teaches them that men aggress and women suffer. Do you want your children to learn this? Also, you are neglecting your children if you permit them to be abused rather than taking them away from the abuse. If you tell your man that you wish to leave him, he may threaten to take your children from you, legally or illegally. Do not let yourself be blackmailed in this way. You have rights that he cannot take away from you. Consult an attorney and get the straight story. Many domestic violence programs provide free or inexpensive legal assistance to those who need it.

Many women are afraid to leave their men because they fear that they will not be able to make it on their own financially. This is a very real consideration. It will be hard for you if he was making most of the money. He will probably tell you about the powerful attorney he will get and how you will be left with nothing if you leave. Most states, however, have laws that protect you to some extent. You will probably be entitled to half of all your combined savings, investments, automobiles, and property. You will probably be entitled to financial support for your children and possibly alimony. The important thing is to not let him scare you into staying. Get an attorney and find out just what the risks will be if you decide to leave. This is very important. You must make a decision of this importance on the basis of accurate information.

If you have never had a job, or maybe only low-paying jobs, it can be intimidating to think about having to support yourself. This is reasonable—you should be nervous! But look around you at all the women who *have* made it on their own. They are no more capable than you are. If they can do it, you can do it. Talk to other divorced women and find out how they managed. You may have to move in with a friend or family member until you get on your feet. This is not the time to be too proud to ask for help. You may have to give up your free time and accept a lower standard of living. Making this big change in your life will not be easy. But in most areas of life, risk is associated with potential benefit.

Many women are reluctant to leave a relationship because they will feel as though they have failed. Remember that it takes two to tango. If you are the one doing all the work to make the relationship happy, your chances of a happy relationship are slim. Under this circumstance, you have not failed by deciding not to throw good money after bad. Rather, there is failure in continuing to beat your head against a wall. A failed marriage is not the same thing as a personal failure, especially if you have done your best.

Now, if you decide that you *can* stay and that there *is* hope for change, good for you! But you must take care of yourself. The first thing that you have to do is find out where he stops and you start. The two of you have probably been too bound up in each other's business for a long time. Start taking care of your own business.

Get some exercise. Aerobic exercise is a quick remedy for depression and stress, and it helps you feel more in control of your life. Get out of the house on a regular basis. Get re-acquainted with your old friends and develop new friendships. A regular night out with the girls may be good for what ails you. Women derive strength from each other in a way that men do not. Take advantage of "the sisterhood." Resist his attempts to isolate you. Keep in touch with your family. Set some goals. To keep you on track, take a piece of paper and write down a one-month plan, a six-month plan, and a one-year plan. Continue your education. Get a job, or a better job. Start doing volunteer work. The point here is that the focus should be on *you* for awhile. Do not continue to let your life revolve completely around him. It will be better for both of you in the long run for there to be two people who share their lives rather than two incomplete people who are joined by their insecurities.

You may want to consider therapy or counseling. Mental health professionals are trained to help you with these issues. They have dealt with many couples who are trying to make a go of it, and they may have some suggestions for you that you would not have considered on your own. Consider getting some individual help as well. You have some growing and changing to do that has nothing to do with your relationship. Besides, there may be things that you want to talk about that you do not wish to share with your man.

But above all, if you decide to work on your relationship, get back in with both feet. Don't make a half commitment, just to "see how it goes." Either get in or get out. Decide what you want and go for it with enthusiasm and effort. The results will be worth it!

20

ON YOUR WAY
you can get more out of life

By this point, you have probably done some soul-searching. Hopefully, you are beginning to see anger as a real issue in your life. Hopefully, you are also beginning to see that it can be controlled. Unbridled male anger does not have to continue to be the pervasive problem to society that it has been for generations. More to the point, you do not have to spend the rest of your life as unhappy as you have been so far.

Remember, there is nothing bad or wrong with anger. Neither is it right or good. It just is. What is good or bad is how your anger affects you and those around you. Too much anger is bad. Too much anger leads to assaults, physical illness, and general unhappiness. You have begun to learn how to deal with the things that make you angry, how to keep your anger in proportion to the circumstances that provoked it, and how to defuse your anger once it erupts. Small annoyances do not have to lead to major tantrums. Insults do not have to lead to fist fights. And most provocations that used to make you angry do not have to lead to anger at all.

Social roles and rules are changing rapidly. You have to be more flexible. You have to learn to roll with the punches and adapt to change. Expand your ideas about what it means to be masculine; the old ways of defining a man, men's work, and masculinity are not in step with the new realities. Economic necessity, the emerging emancipation of women, and other forces dictate that men and women will be sharing duties that were once strictly relegated to one sex or the other. Women will continue to make inroads into business, political institutions, and other seats of power. Men will continue to be called upon to share the load at home. In particular, men will be taking a greater role in raising and caring for their children.

New Rules, New You

New games can be uncomfortable, confusing, and threatening for many men, especially if they keep trying to play by the old rules, the only ones that they have ever learned. While many men will not be happy with these changes at first, the changes are going to occur. If you develop the ability to accept change, you will become more comfortable with an expanded definition of a "man's job." And however you achieve it, if you become more satisfied with yourself, you will be less angry.

One benefit of a greater male presence in the home may be a reversal of the trend for boys to be raised primarily by women. For many generations, boys have grown up without the influence of adult men to teach them what it means to be a man. Many of those boys (ourselves and our sons) have acquired a distorted view of what a man is. For many men, that view includes a gross lack of self-confidence, a view of others as a threat, and an inability to deal comfortably with emotion. Because men have been stunted in their emotional development, they are afraid of their emotions. They have reacted to their emotions by denying them, avoiding them, and becoming angry when feelings are aroused.

The first step in reversing this trend is for the current generation of men to make an investment in their own happiness and then to be willing to make a similar investment in boys. Many men have not learned how to interact comfortably with other people and have reacted by isolating themselves, physically and emotionally. If you start to take some chances with people, you will see that the threat is not as great as it seemed from a distance. The more you socialize and reveal yourself to people, the easier it will become. You can then teach your sons and nephews and brothers to do the same.

Have the courage to acknowledge all of your emotions. Strength has traditionally been thought of a masculine trait. You must develop the strength and the courage to show the world more of yourself than just independence, coolness, and anger. Have the confidence to admit that you are not perfect and never will be. Ask for help sometimes instead of doing everything the hard way. Take little emotional risks every now and then. Let people see other sides of you, the sides that you may have been hiding for fear of ridicule and humiliation. Once you get used to experiencing your emotions, they won't make you so nervous. You won't have to react with anger whenever your emotions are aroused.

Allow others their faults as well. Ease up on your children. The only children who are able to provide perfect and unquestioning obedience are those who are too terrified to act like children. Ease up on your wife or girlfriend, too. It is not her responsibility to make you feel better or agree with you all of the time. Ease up on other people. When they disagree with you, remember that they are not necessarily making any comment about you as a person. Allow yourself to see that there are legitimate viewpoints other than your own.

Be assertive but not aggressive. Say what you need to say in a calm, forthright manner, but avoid hostility. Keep an open mind. Others will not always agree with you; that's the way it should be. Different people have different beliefs and see things their own way. Sometimes you might change your mind and agree with them. Sometimes they might change their minds and agree with you. Sometimes you can agree to disagree. Remember that just because someone disagrees with you, it does not mean that they think you are stupid.

Relax the controls. Let others take the lead sometimes. Your former need to control was based on a fear and distrust of other people and their motives. Try to participate in conversations without dominating them. Stop avoiding parties and other unpredictable situations. Remember that your old attempts to avoid all dependence are different from a healthy independence. All human beings are dependent on others; we all need others to bake the bread, build the cars, and operate the telephone systems. The question is not whether a person is dependent— rather, the question is dependent on whom and for what. To deny your dependence and try to make it absolutely on your own will only invite anger-producing frustration.

Stand up for your principles, but realize that all principles are not equally important. Stiff and rigid pine trees often break in a wind storm, while more flexible palm trees can withstand powerful hurricanes with very little damage. All boxers learn to roll with the punches to minimize the impact. You must learn to adapt your reactions to the circumstances. It is futile to try to get the world to change to fit your ideas of right and wrong. The flexible man has a number of possible responses to challenges. He picks the one that seems best suited to the situation rather than trying to tailor the situation to fit his one stock response.

Learn to anticipate provocative situations and prepare for them. Change the script and rehearse the new reactions that you have developed to deal with frustrating situations. Change your role in the situations that cause you to get angry. It takes two people to have an angry interaction; if you refuse to participate, there will be no argument. If you find ways to keep your anger under control, others will find it less unpleasant to be around you. This will set up a positive cycle of respect and cooperation, replacing the old cycle of competition, saving face, and reciprocal antagonism.

Try to develop clear thinking habits and avoid distorting the information around you. In particular, don't let yourself automatically go to the most negative interpretation of events and things that people say. Remember that you have nothing to apologize for as a human being. You deserve your space on the planet the same as everyone else. Don't be so rigid and judgmental. Try to see the world in shades of gray, instead of black and white. Try to see the humor around you, including in the things that you do.

Be realistic about your attempt to change. It will not happen overnight. You've had many years to get to where you are now. You cannot realistically expect your changes to be instantaneous and complete. You will revert to your old ways from time to time. Others around you may taunt you with this: "You haven't changed a bit." But you *have* changed and you will continue to change, if you put your mind to it. If you lose your temper, or throw a tool, or react in other angry ways, do not give up and decide that your efforts are in vain. Just as golf, cooking, and football take practice, behavior change takes practice too.

Remember to call your attention to your successes as well as your setbacks. When you handle a situation skillfully, without anger, congratulate yourself and take pride in your accomplishment. This might be a good time to go back to Chapter 1 and complete the Anger Scale again. If your score is better, congratulations! If it is not, don't give up. Your efforts will be rewarded eventually.

Above all, remember that change is a natural, unavoidable force. Change is not bad or good; it is inevitable. Trying to avoid change is futile and frustrating. The angry man is faced with three simple choices: 1) to do nothing and remain unhappy; 2) to fight against change, against other people, and against himself, unsuccessfully trying to stay as he is (and despairing as the world changes around him); or 3) embark upon a personally motivated and directed program of personal development— change. You have made the third choice. You have decided to take control of that which is potentially within your control. No one else can do it for you. Good luck!

NOTES

2 THE TROUBLE WITH ANGER

7
"Research indicates that . . . other physical illnesses." R. Williams and V. Williams, *Anger Kills: Seventeen Strategies for Controlling the Hostility That Can Harm Your Health* (New York, NY: HarperPerennial, 1994).

9
"Anger can also express . . . irritable bowel syndrome." Ibid.

10
"Most people convicted . . . more violence as well." *Predictors of Domestic Violence*, available from the National Coalition Against Domestic Violence, P.O. Box 18749, Denver, CO 80218-0749.

14
Novaco Provocation Inventory R. W. Novaco, *Anger Control: The Development and Evaluation of an Experimental Treatment* (Lexington, Mass.: D. C. Heath, 1975).

15 ANGER TURNED INWARD

158
"Recent research is investigating . . . 'anger attacks'" American Psychiatric Association, *Diagnostic and Statistical Manual of Mental Disorders: DSM-IV*, 4th ed. (Washington, D. C.: American Psychiatric Association, 1994).

M. Fava, "Depression with Anger Attacks," *Journal of Clinical Psychiatry* 59, Supp. 18 (1998): 18–22.

M. Fava, and J. F. Rosenbaum. "Anger Attacks in Patients with Depression," *Journal of Clinical Psychiatry* 60, Supp. 15 (1999): 21–24.

M. Fava et al. "Anger Attacks in Depressed Outpatients and Their Response to Fluoxetine," *Psychopharmacology Bulletin* 27, no. 3 (1991): 275–79.

about the author

Thomas J. Harbin, Ph.D., is a clinical psychologist in private practice, specializing in the treatment of angry men. He has written numerous articles for scientific audiences and frequently speaks to groups on the topic of male anger. He lives in North Carolina and enjoys fly-fishing and woodworking in his spare time.